Center Stage

One-Act Plays for Teenage Readers and Actors

Center Stage

One-Act Plays for Teenage Readers and Actors

Edited by

Donald R. Gallo

Harper & Row, Publishers

CENTER STAGE
One-Act Plays for Teenage Readers and Actors

Library of Congress Cataloging-in-Publication Data
Center stage : one-act plays for teenage readers and actors / edited
by Donald R. Gallo.
     p.   cm.
  Summary: A collection of ten one-act plays for teenage actors.
  ISBN 0-06-022170-4. — ISBN 0-06-022171-2 (lib. bdg.)
  1. Young adult drama, American.   2. One-act plays, American.
3. Teenagers—Drama.   [1. Plays—Collections.]   I. Gallo, Donald R.
PS625.5.C46   1990   90-4050
812′.04108—dc20   CIP
                                                            AC

Contents

Acknowledgments

This collection of plays would not exist if it were not for the unconditional acceptance of the concept by Marilyn Kriney after several other publishers had rejected it. And she never would have heard of the concept had Bill Morris not suggested her for a panel of publishers that I was putting together for a conference in 1987. Therefore, to both Bill and Marilyn I am forever grateful.

Thanks are also due to several teachers and their students for reading and reacting to manuscripts being considered for this collection. The opinions of the following people helped shape this collection: Louann Reid and her sophomore writing class at Douglas County (Colorado) High School; Ed Duclos and his students Caroline Goodrow and Jason Pitts at South Windsor (Connecticut) High School; and Joan Ryan and Linda McNair and their second-period theater arts class at Windsor (Connecticut) High School.

Finally, my thanks to Joanna Cotler for her support and guidance throughout the publishing process.

Don Gallo

Introduction

Teenagers have been the main characters in several television series and in numerous movies in recent years. But very few plays—presented on the stage or printed in schoolbooks—have focused on teenagers and their concerns.

That is no longer the case. Here are ten plays that feature teenagers, all of them written specifically for this collection by award-winning authors of novels for young adults. They were written to be performed on the stage or in your classroom, or to be read independently by you in the comfort of your own home. Either way, you are about to enjoy some new views of fictional teenagers in dramatic situations.

Among the one-act plays in this collection you will find a high school girl who has tried to run away from problems at home and must find the strength within herself to carry on; in another play a teenage boy feels torn apart by his parents' problems. On the lighter side, there's disaster-prone Ben Cameron, who has just set a new record by flunking his driving test before his car even leaves the lot, and Cassie Tate, whose unreasonable fears keep her confined to her room in spite of everyone's efforts to lure, bully, trick, and scare her out. *Cages* will force you to think about how we let others determine our destinies. And for something really different, you will be able to participate in the outcome of the final play in this collection by writing your own ending.

As you read these interesting plays, you will be taking part in a unique experiment: There has never before been a collection like this one. Although all these authors have gained fame from their novels and short stories, most had only limited experience writing plays. We reasoned that since dialog was a main ingredient in their fiction, it wouldn't be an impossible task for each of them to write a play.

As you will see, writers like Robin F. Brancato, Alden R. Carter, Dallin Malmgren, Lensey Namioka, Jean Davies Okimoto, and Susan Beth Pfeffer— along with Asher, Forshay-Lunsford, Myers, and Sebestyen—have proved novelists *can* write successful plays for teenagers. Part of the problem was that no one had given them the chance to do so before. I, along with all these new playwrights, hope this collection is the beginning of a trend, that the future will provide more opportunities for novelists to try something new.

Join us in this unprecedented venture as the house lights dim and the curtain is about to rise on Center Stage.

Center Stage

One-Act Plays for Teenage
Readers and Actors

DRIVER'S TEST

by Alden R. Carter

CHARACTERS

BEN CAMERON, sixteen, a high school student. An awkward, gangly kid, he has just failed his driver's test for the second time and is, of course, inconsolable. Normally, he has a sense of humor.

MEGAN CAMERON, thirteen, Ben's sister, a junior high school student. Not in charge of the Cameron household but feels that she should be. Thinks that her driver's test will be a pointless formality. It will be.

PAULINE CAMERON, forty-two, his mother. Harried but trying to keep the sense of humor that has been her best defense against the strains of single parenting.

STAN SCHILLING, sixteen, a friend of Ben's.

DEBBIE BYMERS, sixteen, Ben's love interest. Very pretty, very popular, and too cute by about half. She does not expect to have to walk on a date.

FRED SULLIVAN, forty-five, Pauline's romantic interest.

SETTING

*Most of the stage is taken up with the Camerons'
living room. Upstage right, a swinging door
leads to a kitchen. Downstage right, a door to
outside. At upstage left are two steps and the
hall leading to two or more bedrooms. The door
of the first,* BEN's *room, is visible. Its walls are
opaque under normal light but become trans-
lucent when the lights are turned up within.*

*In living room, a sofa against the back wall
with end table, lamp, and phone beside it, an
easy chair or two, a wastebasket, etc. Mirror
on wall between kitchen and outside doors. In*
BEN's *bedroom, a bed, hanging light fixture,
desk, and chair. The chair must have casters.*

NOTE: This is a comedy, and little should
be played with great seriousness. The director and actors are invited to improvise
at will.

> BEN *enters right through outside door, very upset.* PAULINE *hurries in after him.*

PAULINE: Ben, it's not the end of the world. *(She attempts to put her arms around him.)*

BEN *(whirling away)*: Quit it, Mom!

PAULINE: Come on, Ben. Let's just talk about this for a minute.

BEN *(moving left toward steps)*: There's nothing to talk about, not one darn thing! I blew it. End of discussion.

> *He stumbles slightly on the top step and, trying to keep some dignity, disappears into bedroom, slamming door behind him.* PAULINE *stands for a moment, arms lax, then sighs, takes off coat, and drops it and purse on a chair. She flops on sofa and stares heavenward.*

PAULINE: A mother's hug. You'd think it'd still be worth something. . . .

MEGAN *(entering right from outside)*: So, how'd it go?

PAULINE: He failed.

MEGAN: God, what'd he do this time?

PAULINE *(sighing)*: Pulling out of the lot, he signaled right and turned left.

MEGAN: At the *beginning* of the test?

PAULINE *(nodding)*: Yep. It was some kind of new record, I think.

MEGAN: Well, at least he didn't almost run over a little old lady this time.

PAULINE: It *wasn't* a little old lady. It was a fairly agile adult male, from what I was told.

MEGAN: Whatever. *(Considers.)* Mom, maybe Ben's got some kind of brain problem. You know, not knowing right from left. They call it a dysfunction, I think.

PAULINE *(a little sharply)*: Your brother does not have any kind of brain dysfunction. He just gets nervous, that's all.

MEGAN *(shrugging)*: Well, he's *your* kid, so I guess *you* should know. *(Picks up mother's coat and purse.)* I thought we had a new rule about hanging up coats.

> MEGAN *disappears into kitchen.* PAULINE *makes a face at her back, then stares at the ceiling again, lifting her hands in supplication.*

PAULINE: I mean the hugs used to work. What happened?

Sound of clattering pans from kitchen.

MEGAN *(offstage)*: What's for supper? I'm starved. *(More clattering.)*

PAULINE *(to ceiling)*: I've got a four-wheeled klutz for a son and a kitchen terrorist for a daughter. What did I do wrong, God? I gave them hugs, but they turned into teenagers anyway. *(Turning to kitchen door.)* Fred's taking us out for supper, remember?

MEGAN *(reemerging, hand deep in a bag of potato chips)*: Oh, ya. The big celebration. Well, I'll bet you brother Ben ain't gonna be in the mood.

PAULINE *(rising with a sigh)*: Isn't, not ain't. . . . Well, maybe it'll cheer him up. *(She crosses to BEN's door and knocks.)* Ben? Fred will be here in a little while. Why don't you get ready so we can all go out to eat?

BEN *(from inside)*: No!

PAULINE: Ben, no one's—

BEN: Mother, I am not—repeat *not*—hungry. Now leave me alone!

MEGAN *(between chips)*: I don't think he's hungry, Mom.

PAULINE *(staring at the door a moment, then turning to her daughter)*: Is this really that big a deal?

MEGAN: It's that big a deal, Mom. No license, no car, no dates. I really think you ought to look into this brain-dysfunction thing. I mean, maybe it's kind of like cramps. *(She shoves the bag of chips under her arm and demonstrates, using an imaginary steering wheel.)* He's going along fine until—uh-oh—here's this turn coming up. Then *aarrgghhh!* He gets this incredible charley horse right behind the eyes. *Blinding pain.* He's fighting just to keep it on the road. His hand goes for the turn signal. He can't—

PAULINE *(putting hand on MEGAN's arm)*: Megan—

MEGAN: Huh?

PAULINE *(quietly)*: Shut up or I'll clobber you.

MEGAN: Oh. Okay. Sure. *(PAULINE crosses toward phone. MEGAN rediscovers chips—now well crushed—examines the damage, then resumes eating.)* Clobber? Isn't that kind of hostile, Mom?

PAULINE: It's been a hostile afternoon. Why can't

Ben get dates without a license? Why, I used to walk on a lot—

MEGAN: Right. Through three-foot snowdrifts, too. Hadn't you better get ready before Fred gets here?

PAULINE (*hesitating with phone in hand*): I thought maybe I'd tell him I have to stay home tonight.

MEGAN: Naa, go ahead and go. I'll stay here to make sure Ben doesn't hang himself or anything.

PAULINE (*hesitating a moment longer before hanging up phone*): Well, okay. After today, I really need to get out. (*She crosses left.*) I'm sure Ben just wants a little time to himself.

MEGAN: Mmmmm—

> As PAULINE *exits,* MEGAN *tries the left and right turn signals of her imaginary car, then reaches down for an ignition key, starts her car, and shifts it into gear.*

PAULINE (*offstage*): Sure you don't want to come, dear?

MEGAN: No, thanks. I'm not into partying with old people.

PAULINE (*offstage*): *Old?*

A shoe flies across stage from left wing. MEGAN, *not surprised at its arrival, dodges it neatly. She picks it up and tosses it back down hall.*

MEGAN: I said *older*, Mom. Like, you know, not my age.

She grins, then drives toward kitchen, making a couple of detours around furniture with particular attention to turn signals. Near door she suffers a "brain cramp," crashes into wall, rebounds, and exits right. More clattering in kitchen.

Lights down on main stage. A light goes on in BEN's *room, and we see* BEN *inside through the muslin walls. He is sitting on the bed, head in hands. He rises, paces a moment, then stands gazing at hanging light fixture. He pantomimes hanging himself, giving a little jump while holding an imaginary rope high with one hand. Getting quite carried away with his fantasy, he positions his desk chair under the fixture and tries to mount it. This is tricky, since the chair is on casters. It slides out from under his foot a couple of times, but Ben is determined.*

Spot up on right apron, where we see a happy STAN *dialing a phone. We will not hear* STAN, *only see him talk and react in pantomime.*

The phone in the living room rings. BEN *has finally managed to get a precarious perch atop the chair. He holds his imaginary rope high over head and is about to hop off when the chair slips treacherously from under him. He falls with flailing arms and legs and a tremendous thud. Lights down in* BEN's *room immediately.*

The phone rings a second time. MEGAN *comes in from the kitchen driving with one hand, a plate and sandwich balanced in the other. She brakes hard, glances in the direction of* BEN's *room where there are a few thuds and perhaps a groan as* BEN *rights himself, licks her fingers, and answers the phone.*

MEGAN: Camerons'. . . . Oh, hi, Stan. . . . Pardon? . . . Oh, I get it. He's home *(She looks curiously toward Ben's room, where there is a final thud.)* but the ace driver ain't exactly the ace driver, Stan. He flunked again. . . . *(Stan clutches forehead and pantomimes an exclamation.)* Ya, he blew it on the turn signal pulling out of the lot. Mom thinks he set some kind of speed record for failing. Do you still want to talk to him? . . . Well, maybe that'd be better. . . . What's he going to do about Friday night? I don't know. What's happening Friday night? *(MEGAN listens, then nearly drops plate, but manages to keep it from falling with a long swooping motion.)* Debbie Bymers? . . . No, he didn't tell me. Oh, God, she's way out of his league. And not his type, either. . . . Well, maybe. . . . *(Her face brightens.)* Hey, why don't you guys double or something? I'm not sure I want my brother alone with her anyway. . . . You're delivering pizzas for Laughing Luigi, huh? . . . And Ben was supposed to start delivering pizzas Saturday! . . . *(She collapses in a chair, nearly losing plate again.)* No, he didn't tell me that either. Oh, God, what's he going to do, Stan? . . . *(STAN looks equally worried. Neither of them has much more to say.)* Well, I'll tell him you called, Stan.

They hang up. Light off on STAN. MEGAN *stares in direction of* BEN's *room, very worried.*

PAULINE *(coming in from left)*: Well, I guess I'm ready. Who was that on the phone?

MEGAN *(not looking at her)*: Just Stan. . . . *(PAULINE moves around the room straightening up.)* Mom, he said Ben asked—

The doorbell rings.

PAULINE: There's Fred. Why can't I get that man to use the front door? Sure you don't want to come? *(She exits into kitchen.)*

MEGAN: No, I've already made a sandwich.

> MEGAN *continues to stare in the direction of* BEN's *room.* PAULINE *enters with* FRED. *They don't exactly coo at each other but are close to it. They pause for a moment, talking close.* MEGAN *glances at them in irritation.*

PAULINE: I'll mix us a quick drink and then we'll go.

She hurries off right. Fred sits.

FRED: So how's Megan?

MEGAN: So-so. How're you?

FRED: Now that I'm with your lovely mother, just fine. *(He looks offstage right, fondly.* MEGAN *grimaces.)* So, how's school?

MEGAN: Okay. We pithed frogs today. I like the needle part. Really makes the little suckers squirm. Bisecting is my best subject.

FRED *(still looking toward the kitchen door)*: That's nice. I always liked geometry too. (MEGAN *slaps hand over eyes.* FRED *turns back, making an effort to pay attention to her.)* Got a headache?

MEGAN: No. How about you?

FRED: Me? No. Why?

MEGAN: Just wondering.

An awkward pause.

FRED: So, Ben didn't make out so well, huh?

MEGAN: No. He didn't.

FRED's attention shifts again. MEGAN sits, considering. Lights up in BEN's room. He is trying to smother himself with a pillow. His legs kick frantically, then he pulls pillow from face and sits up gasping. He shakes head in disgust. Lights fade.

MEGAN: Uh, Fred—

FRED: Mmmm . . .

MEGAN: Fred, I just heard that Ben made a date with—

(PAULINE *enters with two drinks.*)

PAULINE: Here you are. Just the way you like it. Would you like something, Megan, dear?

MEGAN: Scotch. And make it a triple, huh?

PAULINE (*sitting and addressing* FRED): Anyway, he's got to wait a month before he can take the test again. I know he's disappointed, but he's taking it way too hard. I mean, it's not the end of the world, is it?

> MEGAN *glances in the direction of* BEN's *room and makes a "well-it-just-might-be" gesture.* FRED *grins, running a hand through his hair.*

FRED: Well, I guess it probably seems like the end of the world to him. . . . It did to me.

PAULINE: *You* failed your driver's test?

FRED: First time. About the worst thing that ever happened to me. When I was a teenager, anyway.

PAULINE: Why, for God's sake? Is this some kind of

male-ego thing? *(Playfully snuggling close.)* I didn't notice you had any macho hang-ups.

MEGAN *(clearing throat)*: I'm still here, guys.

They ignore her and MEGAN *rolls eyes.*

FRED *(laughing indulgently, arm around* PAULINE*)*: Well, there was a little bit of that involved, I guess. Other things got more important later. But it really did hurt. All my friends were getting their licenses on the first try. Even the girls.

PAULINE *(sitting back in mock anger)*: And why *not* the girls?

FRED: That was before liberation. Besides, I had this job in town, and I was sick of listening to my dad grouse about driving me in from the farm.

MEGAN: Uh, Mom, Ben was going to start this job delivering pizzas on Saturday.

PAULINE: What, dear?

MEGAN: Nothing. I'll tell you later.

FRED *(finishing drink)*: Well, are we about set to go?

PAULINE: Anytime you're ready.

They rise and exit right, talking abou... the restaurant.

FRED: Italian sound good?

PAULINE: Sounds marvelous.

FRED: I want to try . . .

MEGAN (*staring in the direction of* BEN's *room again*): Oh God, Ben. How could you be such an idiot?

She rises, crosses left, and hesitates at BEN's *door, fist lifted as if to knock. Then she turns and crosses right and exits to kitchen. Cupboards opening and shutting noisily, sound of a platter dropping. Pause.* BEN's *door opens slowly.* BEN *peeks out, looks both ways, then hurries across stage toward kitchen door. He nearly collides with* MEGAN, *who emerges "driving" fast. She has a tray with a can of soda and a sandwich on it. Dangling from her driving hand is a bag of taco chips.*

MEGAN (*coming to abrupt halt*): Oh . . . hi.

BEN (*angrily*): Not funny, Megan. Definitely not funny.

MEGAN (*calling after him as he disappears into the*

16

kitchen) Hey, I'm just a kid, remember? Like I still get to play at driving a car. Don't take it so personal.

BEN *(offstage)*: I do.

> MEGAN *shrugs, sets tray on a table, produces a can of taco dip from a pocket, and sits.* BEN *reemerges from kitchen with the remains of the bag of potato chips. He digs in, pausing to examine crushed chips suspiciously, then heads for his room.* MEGAN *watches him.*

MEGAN: Stan called.

BEN: Ya, what'd he want?

MEGAN: To say hello, I guess. He told me about your date with Debbie.

BEN *(brought up short, hesitating)*: He did, huh?

MEGAN: Ya. I was kind of surprised.

BEN *(turning to her angrily)*: Why? Surprised she'd go out with me?

MEGAN *(shrugging)*: No, surprised you'd ask her. She's not exactly your type.

BEN: I'm sick of girls my type. I want some fun.

MEGAN: You mean sex.

BEN *(reddening)*: Ya, and what if I do? Something wrong with that?

MEGAN *(shrugging again)*: I guess not, but I still don't think she's your type.

BEN *(exasperated)*: Well, why not? The way I see it, she's got everything.

MEGAN: Except a brain maybe.

BEN *(sneering)*: You should talk.

> *He heads for his room.* MEGAN *seems about to say something but makes a face at him instead, pantomiming steering and using a turn signal. A little of the taco dip spills.* BEN *shuts door behind him.* MEGAN *wipes taco dip from pants with a finger and licks it.*

MEGAN *(musing)*: I just don't want you to get hurt, Big Brother. *(She looks toward his room, her face suddenly pained.)* God, you're beat up enough already. *(Suddenly, she spots the tray with soda and sandwich.)* Hey, Ben——*(She hops up and takes the tray to his door.)* Ben, I made you a sandwich.

BEN: I'm not hungry. Go away.

MEGAN: Ben, Debbie's not going to want to walk. What are you going to do?

BEN: Maybe I'll just kill myself. *Go away.*

MEGAN (*after hesitating a long moment*): Well, I'm leaving your sandwich and pop outside just in case you want to eat first. Answer the phone, huh? I'm going to take a shower and then go over to Marcia's.

> *She exits left. Slight pause. Sound of a shower turned on.* BEN's *door opens and a hand reaches out, grabs half of the sandwich, and disappears. A few seconds later, the hand reappears, feeling for the can of soda but knocking it over. The can bounces down steps. Explosive groan from* BEN. *He pokes head out, looks quickly down hall to left, then hurries to retrieve can. He gives a sigh of relief to find it unopened. He starts to cross to kitchen, then turns back to retrieve second half of sandwich, stumbling slightly on the steps again and slamming the can hard on the top step. He is halfway across living room again when the doorbell rings. He freezes. After a long moment, he circles room, creeping close enough to peek through curtain*

on the front door. He pulls back quickly, plas-
tering himself against the wall.

BEN (to himself): Oh, my God! Not her! (The doorbell
rings again. He sets down the can of soda on a table,
takes a deep breath, and opens door.) Debbie! What
are you doing here?

> DEBBIE enters. She is dressed seductively in
> light-colored blouse and corduroy slacks. Her
> hair is perfect, of course.

DEBBIE (drawling in ever-so-cute voice): Why, I just
came by to see my guy. (Approaching close, toying
with his shirtfront) I've been thinking about you all
day, and I just couldn't stay away. Did you get the
concert tickets?

BEN: Uh, ya. Well, reservations, that is. I've got to
pick them up Friday.

DEBBIE: I am so looking forward to Friday night. I
just adore Ruptured Chicken. They are the best
band. (She plucks at one of his shirt buttons and gives
his chest a light caress.) We are going to have the
best time.

> She smiles seductively; then, duty done, she
> moves right, surveying the contents of the room.

BEN (*thoroughly unhinged*): Uh, right. Nice day, huh? (*Debbie makes a "Mmmmm . . ." sound of agreement as she checks out the furniture.*) Hey, did you see that there's a Stephen King movie playing at the Hollywood? Want to see it?

DEBBIE: Maybe sometime.

BEN: Well, maybe we ought to see it Friday. The Hollywood's close. We could even walk.

DEBBIE (*laughing*): Stop teasing me. I wouldn't miss Ruptured Chicken for anything.

BEN (*doggedly*): Well, I like Ruptured Chicken too, but it's going to be kind of a long drive, and I'm not sure I'll have the gas money. You see, I thought I had this job delivering pizzas for Laughing Luigi, but now—

DEBBIE (*turning, with a big but mildly challenging smile*): Well, if you don't think I'm worth it . . .

BEN (*fumbling*): Well, sure you are. You're worth, uh, you know, anything. It's just—

DEBBIE (*overwhelming smile*): You're sweet. (*All business*) When are you going to pick me up?

> Slight pause. BEN *tries to gather thoughts.* DEBBIE *resumes inspection of room, stopping*

*to straighten a picture. In the background the
sound of the shower ceases.*

BEN: Debbie, I gotta tell—

DEBBIE *spots the can of pop* BEN *left on the
table and snatches it up.*

DEBBIE: Hey, I'm really thirsty. Can I drink this?

BEN: Sure. I mean, no! Don't—

He lunges for the can, but it is too late. DEBBIE
*pops the top and gets a gusher in the face and
over her hair. She screams. The can runs over,
and they fumble wildly for some place to put
it. An end table is overturned.* DEBBIE *does a
good deal of yelping as she pleads with* BEN *to
"do something."* BEN *tries to get a wastebasket
positioned under the can, but* DEBBIE *is not
good under pressure and fails to get the idea.
In the middle of their flailing about,* BEN *starts
laughing. Finally, he gets hold of the can and
dumps it in the wastebasket.*

DEBBIE *(looking at her sticky hands and stained blouse)*:
Uuuggghh. God, what did you do? Shake it up?
(With very angry look) And what are you laughing
at, turkey?

BEN (*trying to hide grin*): Sorry. I, uh, I dropped it. I was just getting a different one. Hold on a second; I'll find you a towel.

DEBBIE: *You* hold on a second. Just what do you think is so darn funny?

BEN: Nothing, nothing. It just seemed kind of funny for a second. You know, the way we——

DEBBIE: I don't see *anything* funny about it! This is a new blouse, I'll have you know. I get all dressed up to come and see you, and what happens? You squirt Coke all over my clothes and — Oh God, my hair! (*She runs to mirror, letting out a groan when she sees the damage. She's almost crying.*) Oh, God. I just fixed it. It'll take me hours to get it right again. Oh, God.

BEN: I'm sorry, Debbie. It looks okay. Really.

DEBBIE (*fussing with hair*): Oh, God. What a mean trick. What do you do at Halloween? Put ground glass in the candy?

BEN: No, razor blades.

DEBBIE: Don't make jokes! This isn't the least bit funny! If you hadn't——

23

BEN: Debbie, I didn't exactly squirt Coke all over you. I tried to stop you—

DEBBIE: Are you telling me it *wasn't* your fault? You just shake the heck out of a can of pop and leave it lying around for anybody to open. And little old me just happens to be the first one by. That's a pretty rotten thing to do, if you ask me—

BEN: Debbie, I didn't do it on purpose. It was an accid—

DEBBIE: Just get the towel, huh?

BEN: Ya, sure.

He exits through swinging door to kitchen.

DEBBIE *(pulling out a comb and working furiously at her hair)*: If it wasn't that I really wanted to see Ruptured Chicken, I'd—

BEN *(reappearing)*: Here. I brought you a wet one and a dry one.

DEBBIE *(sarcastically)*: Thank you very much.

She starts daubing at blouse and slacks. BEN watches, again having to hide a smile. MEGAN enters left, tucking blouse into blue jeans. She

*looks at strange scene in confusion, perhaps
even looking in the direction of the audience
for an explanation. She takes a step back to
eavesdrop on* BEN *and* DEBBIE.

BEN: Debbie—

DEBBIE *(sharply)*: What?

BEN: I think I'd better tell—

DEBBIE: Oh, this is hopeless! *(Turning on him.)* A new
blouse and cords just ruined. And all because—

BEN: Debbie, you're being dumb. The stains will
come out in the wash—

DEBBIE *(furious)*: Dumb! You call *me* dumb? I didn't
shake up that can of pop and leave it—

BEN: Oh, just stop it, Debbie. Now, I'm sorry. Really
sorry. I guess I should have moved faster. Maybe
I shouldn't have left it there in the first place.

DEBBIE: *Maybe?*

BEN: Okay, okay, I shouldn't have left it sitting
there. But jeez, it's not the end of the world.

DEBBIE: Maybe not, but you had no right to laugh
at me!

BEN: I wasn't laughing at you. I've had this kind of tough day, and it just hit me as kind of funny. That's all.

DEBBIE *(arms akimbo, very sarcastic)*: Oh, so now I'm supposed to feel sorry for poor little Ben after his tough day?

BEN: I failed my driver's test again, Debbie.

DEBBIE *(thunderstruck)*: You flunked *again*?

BEN *(levelly)*: Yep. Set the speed record too, I think.

DEBBIE: Well, isn't that just great! Now how are we supposed to get to the concert?

BEN: I guess we're not. I'm sorry.

DEBBIE: I'm not interested in how sorry you are! I turned down two other dates for a chance to see Ruptured Chicken. And now you can't get me there!

BEN: It doesn't look like it, but we can still walk to the movies.

DEBBIE *(hurling towels at him)*: Not a chance! *(Heads for door, then whirls.)* And don't call me again, you jerk.

*She exits through front door, slamming it behind
her. At the crash of the door,* MEGAN *gives a
little jump and quickly exits left.* BEN *stands
for a long moment with the towels in his hands,
then begins wiping the spilled pop from the
floor. Suddenly, he begins to giggle. He pantomimes the explosion of the can and the frenzy
following.*

BEN *(to himself)*: God, I wish I had a videotape of
that.

*He rises, tosses towels through the kitchen door,
and flops in a chair. He giggles again, then
puts his head in his hands, unsure if he should
laugh or cry. After a long moment, he sits back
and stares at nothing. Then slowly his hands
reach out. He works an imaginary turn signal
a couple of times, then twists an imaginary
ignition key and begins driving. As he begins
to get into the spirit of his fantasy, he tries to
scoot chair forward. It resists. He tries again,
then gives up and lets hands fall in his lap.
He sits motionless for a moment, then has an
inspiration. He hops up, pushes chair and other
furniture back, then hurries to his room. He
reappears with his chair, makes his way carefully*

*down steps, and positions it at the center of
the living room. He takes a deep breath, opens
car door, sits, and begins to drive in earnest.
Rolling around the furniture, he carefully signals each turn. ("Left . . . okay. Now a right.
That's it.") MEGAN reappears at the top of
the steps. She watches him for a moment, then
turns quickly and exits left again. In a moment
she is back with a similar chair. BEN has just
maneuvered so that he is facing left. He sees
her and freezes in embarrassment.*

BEN: I thought you'd gone to Marcia's.

MEGAN: I hadn't left yet. . . . *(She looks down at her
chair.)* Can I ride with you? *(BEN hesitates.)* Please?

BEN: Ya, I guess. Come on. *(She puts chair beside his.)*
No backseat driving, huh?

MEGAN: I promise. But kind of tell me what we're
going to do, okay?

BEN: Okay. Let's get out of this parking place first.

*They start maneuvering, quickly getting the
hang of working together. As they speed up,
they begin giggling, then laughing as their*

motoring becomes faster and a bit reckless. Spontaneous exchange, e.g.:

MEGAN: Watch out for that little old lady!

BEN: Whoops. Okay, we missed her.

MEGAN (*looking over shoulder*): Jeez, she dropped her bags.

BEN: Fire trucks coming, got to pull over.

MEGAN: Follow them; I want to see the fire.

They move as fast as they can across stage, finally running out of gas and breath.

MEGAN (*laughing breathlessly, then turning serious*): Ben, when I'm old enough, will you teach me how to drive?

BEN: You can find somebody better.

MEGAN: No, you're going to be great.

BEN (*looking at her hard*): Do you really believe that?

MEGAN: Yes, I really do.

BEN (*grunting, embarrassed*): Well, I suppose I could try. . . . Hey, I'm hungry.

MEGAN *(pointing toward kitchen door)*: There's a McDonald's up ahead.

BEN: Well, let's go. *(They roll toward door.)* Shall we run through the drive-up or eat inside?

MEGAN: Let's go in. *(They stop and rise, making a show of opening the car doors.)* Don't forget the keys.

BEN: Not a chance. Nobody's going to steal *my* wheels. *(*MEGAN *exits.* BEN *stops for a moment, looking back at his "car." He polishes a spot on the hood with a shirt sleeve, then stands back to admire his work.)* Next time, baby.

> *He smiles and, with his left hand working a turn signal, exits.*

CURTAIN

ALDEN R. CARTER

Alden Carter says he "suffered terminal stage fright in junior high school and never participated in another play." Thus *Driver's Test* is Carter's first theater work since junior high school.

When he began to write for publication, after serving in the Navy, trying his hand as a land developer, and teaching high school English and journalism, he concentrated on both fiction and nonfiction aimed at teenagers.

Al Carter's young adult novels have all been prize winners, named Best Books for Young Adults by the American Library Association. *Growing Season*, his first novel, about a city boy whose parents buy a farm, was followed by *Wart, Son of Toad*, which explores the relationship between a teenage boy and his father, an unpopular science teacher in the same high school. *Sheila's Dying* is about a boy and a girl who help their friend Sheila face an inevitable death from cancer. The experiences of an angry teenager sent away from his alcoholic mother to live with relatives on a farm in upstate Wisconsin are the focus of *Up Country*. All of Carter's novels provide sensitive portrayals of the joys and struggles of teenage life. His latest novel is called *Robodad*.

Among his nonfiction works are *Supercomputers*; *Modern Electronics*; *Radio: From Marconi to the Space Age*; books about Illinois and modern China; a series about the American Revolution, including *Colonies in Revolt* and *At the Forge of Liberty*; and other historical works, including *Last Stand at the Alamo*, *Shoshoni*, and *The Battle of Gettysburg*.

He lives in Marshfield, Wisconsin, with his wife and two children.

WORLD AFFAIRS

by Susan Beth Pfeffer

CHARACTERS

TERRY, a fifteen-year-old girl

DANNY, Terry's boyfriend

LIZ, Terry's best friend

MOTHER

SETTING

A bare stage. At the back, stage center, is a table with a telephone. Standing next to it is MOTHER. *In the front, stage right, is another table and telephone.*

TERRY *enters, walks to the stage-right table, and smiles apologetically to the audience.*

TERRY: This is mostly about me. Sorry about that. I'm only fifteen, so the thing I know best about is me. I'm taking world history in school, but I'm still not an expert in world affairs.

I guess since this is about me, I should tell you some stuff about myself. Kind of an introduction. My name is Terry, and I'm fifteen—well, I told you that—and I live here, in this house, with my father and mother. My brother used to live here— his name is Rich—but he's a freshman in college, and he lives away from home. It's been almost six months since he left. At the beginning I missed him, but now I'm used to it.

My father's an accountant. He's a whiz with numbers. At least that's what my mother always says. "Your father is a whiz with numbers." Dad still laughs when she says it, but I think that's more because it's a family joke than because it's really funny. I don't know what's so funny about it anyway, whiz with numbers. Not that it matters. Right now I'm just thinking about everything my mother ever said, and trying to make sense of it. That doesn't mean everything makes sense, or ever did, or ever will.

That's my mom back there (TERRY *gestures toward* MOTHER). She sells real estate. Last week she sold five houses. We live in Willow Grove. Willow Grove's the kind of place you could call Willow Grove, USA. Mom says it's a perfect suburb. My brother played in Little League. I was a Girl Scout. We went trick-or-treating every Halloween. Mom made us costumes. I used to like to go as a princess. One year Mom made a crown for me out of construction paper and sparkles, and by the time I was ready to go trick-or-treating, all the sparkles had fallen off, so Mom made a whole new crown for me. It was yellow and the sparkles were silver, and she said I was the prettiest princess in the world. Dad said so too, but Mom said it first, and she was the one who made two crowns for me. That's why this is all so hard. Because I love my mom so.

> MOTHER *picks up the telephone. We can see that she is talking and enjoying the conversation, but we cannot hear her words.*

I came home from school and I remembered I was supposed to meet Danny. He's my boyfriend. Well, he was my boyfriend, until all this happened. Anyway, I was running late and I figured it would be best if I called him up and canceled. We were just going to study math together. It was no big deal to cancel. I picked up the phone to call him, and I could hear Mom's voice on the extension.

MOTHER: Yes, darling. I know just how you feel.

TERRY: Mom doesn't call Dad "darling." She calls him "hon" and "Dad" and "a whiz with numbers." But she doesn't call him "darling."

MOTHER: No, I didn't hear anybody pick up the phone. Darling, what are you worrying about? I haven't heard Terry come home from school yet. And Jack would never do that. First of all, he doesn't suspect a thing. And secondly he's not the kind of man who'd bug his own phone.

TERRY: Jack's my father. The whiz.

MOTHER: I know, darling. I think about you all the time too. Sometimes at night Jack and Terry watch TV, and I just walk off, go into the kitchen, and think about how much I want you. I can't bear to be in the same room with him when I start thinking of you that way. Not that he would notice. You know Jack. He's a whiz with numbers, but not much else.

TERRY: What was I supposed to do? If I hung up the phone, Darling would be sure to hear. So I held on. I stopped breathing though. I remember that, how funny it was I no longer needed to breathe.

MOTHER: I really should get off. Terry'll be home from school any minute now. Yes, tomorrow. I'm meeting a client at two, so we'll have a couple of hours. Think of me until then. Think of me at least once. *(MOTHER hangs up the phone.)*

TERRY: I may not have needed to breathe, but I definitely needed fresh air. I hung up the phone and ran outside.

MOTHER: Terry? Terry, are you home?

TERRY: Five minutes before, I'd been outside, and the only thing I'd noticed were the daffodils just starting to stick their heads out. Now I noticed everything. My house, and how thin its walls were, how fragile its foundation. It could never survive an earthquake or a tornado or a jet airplane crashing into it. My mother's in real estate. You'd think she would have bought us a house that could survive a disaster.

I started to cry. You'd cry too, if your house

were so weak and sickly. I really expected a jet to crash in right then and destroy my home. I'm still surprised one didn't.

> TERRY *stands center stage, silently weeping. She doesn't notice* DANNY *crossing stage left and joining her.*

DANNY: Ter? What's the matter? Is everything okay?

> TERRY, *startled, edges away from* DANNY.

DANNY: Terry, what it it? Did somebody hurt you?

TERRY: Go away.

DANNY: Not until you tell me what's the matter.

TERRY *(to audience)*: What a mess. I mean, what was I supposed to say? "Go away, Danny. My house can't survive if a jet airplane crashes into it"?

TERRY *(to* DANNY*)*: Go away, Danny. My house can't survive if a jet airplane crashes into it.

DANNY: That's what you're crying about? Terry, no jet airplane is going to crash into your house. The odds must be a zillion to one against it.

TERRY *(to audience)*: That's Danny for you. A whiz

with numbers. I could tell right away that approach wasn't going to work.

DANNY: Terry, please, I want to know what's wrong.

TERRY (*to* DANNY): What would you do if you found out one of your parents was having an affair?

DANNY: Are you crazy? My parents? They had sex three times, once for each of my brothers and once for me.

TERRY: Just because they don't have sex with each other doesn't mean they don't have sex with other people.

DANNY: Dad's too scared of AIDS. And Mom's too scared of getting her hair mussed.

TERRY (*to audience*): The problem is I know Danny's parents. They would never have affairs. There was no point asking Danny.

DANNY: You still haven't given me an answer. What's wrong Terry? Why are you crying?

TERRY (*to* DANNY): I never want to see you again.

DANNY: What?

TERRY: You heard me. I hate you. I want you to leave.

DANNY: What did I do? I just got here, and you were crying, and all I asked was what's the matter. You can't hate me for that.

TERRY: I hate you for other things.

DANNY: What other things?

TERRY: I know you asked Monica out on a date.

DANNY: Monica? Are you crazy? I don't even like Monica.

TERRY: See! You didn't ask Monica out just because you don't like her. That means you'll ask Janice out or Chrissy. You like them. You've told me so often enough.

DANNY: What if I do like them? What if I do ask them out sometime? I haven't yet, so what are you making such a big fuss over?

TERRY: If you can't understand it, then I can't explain it to you.

DANNY: I don't get it. I come on over here to work on math with you—we do have that test tomorrow, remember—and instead you start screaming at me about asking girls out. It doesn't make sense.

MOTHER *picks up phone.*

MOTHER: Sometimes at night Jack and Terry watch TV, and I just walk off, go into the kitchen, and think about how much I want you.

TERRY *(to audience)*: That's my kitchen she was talking about. The church had a bake sale last year, and I baked cookies in that very kitchen. Dad drinks his coffee there every morning. You remember Dad. He's the one she doesn't call "Darling."

DANNY: Maybe it's PMS. My mother goes crazy when she has PMS.

TERRY *(to* DANNY*)*: That does it. Go away. I won't have anything to do with a boy who thinks he can cheat on me and then claims it's all my hormones' fault.

DANNY: All right. I'm gone. Give me a call if you ever become human. (DANNY *walks offstage left.*)

TERRY *(to audience)*: I watched Danny walk away from me, and I wanted to call out to him, beg him to come back.

MOTHER *(into telephone)*: Think of me until then. Think of me at least once.

TERRY: But I just watched him walk away. It isn't like Danny and I are really close. We've dated a few times, gone to movies, to parties, together. We've kissed, but not much more. So what was I giving up? Nothing, really. And I couldn't trust him. How could I know who he spoke to on the phone when he thought nobody else was home?

MOTHER *hangs up the phone.*

MOTHER: Terry? Terry, are you home?

TERRY: I wasn't ready to go back in. I wasn't sure I'd ever be ready. You think you know a house, a kitchen, but then you find out you don't. When you find that out, you don't want to go back in. So I decided to go to my friend Liz's place. Liz's place is safe. It gave up having secrets a long time ago.

TERRY *crosses the stage and pantomimes knock-ing on door.* LIZ *enters from stage left and walks to* TERRY.

LIZ: Hi, Terry. What's up?

TERRY: Nothing. Does something have to be up for me to visit? We've been friends for ten years now, Liz. I was there for you in second grade when you wet your pants during the thunderstorm and Marshall Melmeyer called you a scaredy-cat. Why can't I just drop by for a visit? Since when do I need a reason?

LIZ: Sorry. I just thought you had a date with Danny.

TERRY: It wasn't a date. We were going to do our math homework together. That's not my idea of a date. A date is when a boy picks a girl up and takes her someplace nice, someplace special. Dates involve food and money and social activities, not doing math homework. Besides, he doesn't like my hormones, and I don't much care for his.

LIZ: That'll do it. Are we going to stand here in the doorway, or are you coming in?

TERRY (to audience): It was funny. All the way to Liz's I could picture what her living room looked like, how it would feel to sit on her sofa and tell her about Mom. But once I got there, I found I couldn't cross the threshold.

TERRY (to LIZ): I'd rather stand here.

LIZ: Fine.

TERRY: It's your mother's sofa. It's too pink. I don't

think I could stand sitting on a sofa that pink right now.

LIZ: You're not the first person to have that reaction. Mom says all her life she dreamed of having a pink sofa, but now that she does, it's making her reevaluate all her other life's dreams.

TERRY: Do you think your mother ever cheated on your father?

TERRY *(to audience)*: What was I to do? I couldn't talk about sofas all day long.

LIZ *(Looks long and hard at* TERRY*)*: What do you mean by cheating?

MOTHER *(into telephone)*: You know Jack. He's a whiz with numbers, but not much else.

TERRY *(to* LIZ*)*: What do you think I mean? Cheating. How many varieties does it come in?

LIZ: Look, the day Dad moved out on Mom and me, he moved into his girlfriend's house. I don't think he would have done that if he was still just at the handshake level with her, do you?

TERRY: I didn't ask about your father. I asked about your mother.

LIZ: That's my point. Maybe my mom had an affair toward the end—I don't know. I wouldn't blame her if she did. Not with Dad spending every spare minute, and a few he couldn't spare, with his girlfriend. Is that cheating? If Dad was screwing around for years, and Mom had an affair or two toward the end, who was she cheating on? Daddy? Vows don't count if they're one-sided.

TERRY: So your mother did have affairs.

LIZ: I didn't say that. I said I'd understand if she had. What is this? Some kind of Harris poll? How many suburban mothers are unfaithful this week? Plenty. You can count on it.

TERRY *(to audience)*: How about that? Liz was a whiz with numbers too. I'm surrounded by statisticians.

LIZ: Terry, I know the sofa is awfully pink, but I still think maybe you should come in for a few minutes. You don't look so great.

TERRY *(to LIZ)*: Liz, before your father moved out, when you must have known things were bad, did you ever look at your house? I mean really look at it, to see how strong it was, how firm its foundation?

LIZ: I was nine years old. I looked at my bedroom. I counted all my dolls. Every night I did that, counted them one by one. I had seventeen big dolls and another twelve little ones. Sometimes I'd take all my dolls, the seventeen big ones and the twelve little ones, and I'd carry them into the closet. And when they were all there, I'd go in the closet too, and close the door and sit in the dark surrounded by my dolls. I was right, too. When Dad moved out, and we had to sell the house, Mom said I couldn't take all my dolls with me, there wouldn't be room for them all in the apartment. She let me keep a half dozen big ones and four of the little ones. Not that it mattered by then. I was ten already and was outgrowing dolls. But they sure had kept me company in the closet those nights.

TERRY: Liz, I'm scared. I'm so scared.

LIZ: Your mother? Are you sure?

TERRY *nods.*

LIZ: You're going to have to go back at some point.

You can't spend the rest of your life outside my door.

TERRY: But what should I say to her?

LIZ: Tell her the truth. Or lie. Tell her you know, or don't tell her anything at all.

TERRY: And what do I say to my father?

LIZ: When you know what to say to your mother, then you'll know what to say to him too.

> TERRY *and* LIZ *embrace.* LIZ *walks offstage, while* TERRY *crosses back to center stage.*

TERRY *(to audience)*: I love Liz. She understands so much so quickly. But frankly, she could have been a little more specific with her advice. Tell, don't tell, truth, lies. All *that* I could have figured out for myself.

When I got back to the house, I could feel my mother inside it.

> MOTHER *walks around house, putting things away, starting to cook supper.*

I used to love to come home as a kid, and find Mom inside. It was as though she only came alive when I got home from school. I don't know if

Rich felt that way. The day he went off to college though, she cried.

TERRY *stands very still in front of house.*

I guess it was silly of me thinking of her that way, only alive when I was around. I knew different. I knew better. When I was in school, that was when she made my Halloween costumes. That was when she bought the milk and the eggs and the sparkles. That was when she planted the daffodils.

I know I'll have to go in. Sooner or later, I'll have to go in. We don't even have a pink sofa for me to use as an excuse.

And when I do, we'll talk and I'll say something. Maybe it'll be about school. Maybe it'll be about affairs. Maybe it'll be about how much I loved her when she said I was the prettiest princess in the world.

TERRY *enters house.*

MOTHER: Terry. Terry, are you home?

TERRY: Yes, Mom. I'm here.

CURTAIN

SUSAN BETH PFEFFER

Following her triumphant lines "Fireman, fireman, save my child," in her second-grade play, Susan Beth Pfeffer was frequently cast in major parts in school plays, culminating in her giggling her way through the lead role in *The Princess That Couldn't Laugh*. Her acting experience peaked when she played Eeyore in a musical production of *Winnie-the-Pooh* held on Senior Citizens' Day at the Orange County (New York) Fair. The senior citizens, she says, were nonplussed.

Sensing that stardom was not in her future, Susan Beth Pfeffer wrote a children's play entitled *A Witch in Time*. The handful who saw it mostly remember it for the musical number "Oh How I Hate to Leave Ho-ho-kus." After that she limited her theatrical experience to buying tickets and seeing the show. Until, that is, she wrote *World Affairs*.

Now a resident of Middletown, New York, Pfeffer has written reviews, articles, children's books—including *What Do You Do When Your Mouth Won't Open?* and *Courage, Dana!*—and novels for teenagers. Among her young adult novels are *Beauty Queen*, *Marly the Kid*, *A Matter of Principle*, *Fantasy Summer*, and *Getting Even*, along with two series: *Make Me a Star*, about a group of young actors in a TV show called *Hard Time High*, and more recently *The Sebastian Sisters*.

Her novel about teenage suicide, *About David*, was named an American Library Association Best Book for Young Adults, as was *The Year Without Michael*, the moving story about what happens to a family when one of the children disappears and is never heard from again.

Susan Beth Pfeffer's most recent novel is a story about adoption entitled *Most Precious Blood*.

HERBAL
NIGHTMARE

by *Lensey* *Namioka*

CHARACTERS

AMANDA LIU, a Chinese-American teenager

KATHY

JEFF

TONY

LEILA

} Amanda's classmates

OLD CHINESE WOMAN

GHOST OF OPERA SINGER

SETTING

The front room of Liu's Medicine Shop, a store in Chinatown selling Chinese medicines. A counter is placed parallel to the back wall of the room, and on it is a row of paper boxes containing various scraps of dried materials. Behind the counter is a buffet. The lower part of the buffet is a bureau with small drawers, and the upper part consists of shelves. Sitting on the shelves are large glass jars containing unfamiliar-looking lumps. A table is in the middle of the room. A few pieces of white paper lie on the table, each with a heap of assorted medicinal herbs on it. Also on the table is an abacus and a set of Chinese balance scales with small brass weights. A metal scoop lies next to the balance scale. To the right of the table are several upright wooden chairs. A floor lamp stands beside the counter. A door on the right side of the room leads to the back of the house, and a door on left side leads to the street. Outside this door, on the left apron, is a bus stop.

SCENE 1

TIME: *Early evening.*

AT CURTAIN'S RISE: AMANDA LIU *is preparing packages of mixed medicinal herbs. She folds up the paper around the small heaps of medicines on the table and tucks in the corners. Taking out a felt pen, she labels the packages one by one. She puts the small packets of wrapped medicine on the counter and spreads several more sheets of paper on the table. From one of the boxes on the counter, she scoops out a quantity of herbs and weighs it with the balance scale. She adds a little more, weighs it again, and pours it onto one of the sheets of paper. She does this with the other sheets of paper, and starts to repeat the process with herbs from another box. Before she can finish weighing the second batch of herbs, the door to the outside opens.* JEFF *and* KATHY *come in.*

KATHY: Hi, Amanda.

AMANDA: Oh, hi, Kathy. So you and Jeff decided to come after all. What about the others?

KATHY: Tony said he'll be over as soon as he finishes

his football practice. And Leila, of course, wants to come with Tony. I hope we aren't interrupting something important.

AMANDA: This is okay. We're closing pretty soon. In fact, my parents are gone for the day.

> JEFF *is walking around the medicine store, looking curiously at the unfamiliar objects. At the mention of* TONY *and* LEILA, *he stops and goes over to* KATHY.

JEFF: Football practice nothing. I bet Tony's going to chicken out.

AMANDA: Why would Tony want to come anyway, Jeff? He's a football jock, and a Chinese medicine store isn't his scene.

JEFF: Tony's always trying to impress people about how he likes to take risks, see.

AMANDA *(puzzled)*: He doesn't have to impress anybody. The girls are crazy about Tony already. Look at Leila.

KATHY: It's not the girls Tony's trying to impress. He hangs around with a bunch of boys who are always teasing him about being so straight. Tony is keen on getting an athletic scholarship, so he doesn't want to get into anything that spoils his chances.

JEFF: I was getting a little tired of listening to Tony's talk, so I decided to call his bluff.

AMANDA: What do you mean, Jeff?

JEFF: I heard you telling Kathy about your parents' medicine store, and it gave me an idea. I told Tony and Leila that you can probably get high on some of those Chinese drugs, and I challenged him to try some. *(He peers eagerly into the boxes on the counter.)* I wonder what some of these things can do.

> *The two girls draw away from* JEFF *and speak to each other in low voices.*

AMANDA *(looking reproachfully at* KATHY*)*: I don't get to make many friends, since I have to come here right after school every day and work in the shop. You're almost my only friend, Kathy, and I invited you over today because you said you were really interested in seeing the place where I work. But you only came to get some excitement out of Chinese herbs, didn't you?

KATHY *(quickly)*: That's not true, Amanda. I'm really interested in your parents' shop. Only, Jeff had this idea about having fun with Chinese medicines, and Tony said he'd come because Jeff dared him to. (*She glances at* JEFF, *who is over at the counter, examining the contents of the boxes.*) And Leila always follows Tony.

AMANDA: Leila's got a crush on Tony. Everybody knows that.

KATHY *(still softly)*: The trouble is, Amanda, Jeff likes Leila a lot, even though she never looks at anyone except Tony. So I want to make sure Jeff doesn't try something real crazy just to impress her.

AMANDA *(looking earnestly at* KATHY*)*: You like Jeff, don't you?

KATHY *(embarrassed)*: Well . . . I know he can be a pest, but he's fun and he has some great ideas. I don't want him to get into trouble.

The door to the street opens, and TONY *and* LEILA *enter.*

TONY: Hi, everybody. Sorry we're late. Had a bit of trouble finding your place, Amanda.

LEILA *(shivering a little)*: Brr. . . . You know, it's cold and dark in here. *(Looks contemptuously around.)* This place is kind of creepy. I can write a story, you know, for my English III assignment and call it *The Haunted Medicine Shop.*

AMANDA *(quietly)*: Some people say the shop *is* haunted, Leila.

TONY *(eagerly)*: No kidding? Who's haunting the place?

AMANDA *(after a pause)*: The ghost of an elderly Chinese man who died. He drank some medicine here in the store and had a heart attack. *(Pointing to one of the wooden chairs)* He was sitting right there when it happened.

> *The others hastily draw away from the chair, and* LEILA *gives a little scream.*

LEILA: What . . . what did the ghost look like?

AMANDA: The old man was an actor in an opera troupe, and his ghost supposedly appears in full costume. I've never seen him myself, but my mother caught sight of him once. He was dressed all in black, and his face was dead white, she said.

TONY: A Chinese ghost! That's great! And an opera singer, even.

LEILA *(trying to laugh)*: You know, that's all we need: a Chinese ghost that goes, "Figaro, Figaro!"

> JEFF *tries to show* LEILA *something, but she ignores him at first. He finally catches her attention and points to one of the glass jars.*

JEFF: Hey, look, Leila! It's a piece of snakeskin!

LEILA *(shuddering)*: O-o-h, gross! *(Turning to* AMANDA*)* What is snakeskin supposed to cure? Warts?

AMANDA *(embarrassed)*: I'm afraid I don't know what we use the snakeskin for. . . .

TONY: For snake oil, of course! Don't all quack medicine men sell snake oil?

JEFF *(picking up something from one of the paper boxes)*: Say, this looks like a deer antler. *(He picks up something from another box.)* And look, dried sea horses!

AMANDA: Some of the stuff is just for show, and we don't take them seriously anymore. Like our powdered rhinoceros horn, for instance.

JEFF *(eagerly)*: I know what rhino horn is used for. It's an aphrodisiac, isn't it?

TONY: What's an afro . . . Whatever it is?

JEFF *(delighted to score off* TONY*)*: If you have to ask, Tony, you're too young to know. *(He glances at* LEILA, *but she just shrugs.)*

AMANDA: An aphrodisiac, Tony, is supposed to make you feel more sexy.

TONY *(grinning)*: A horn to make you horny—no wonder Jeff is so keen! I wouldn't have to bother. *(*LEILA *snickers.)*

KATHY *(feeling sorry for* JEFF *and joining the others at the counter)*: It must be awfully expensive stuff, if you have to kill a whole rhinoceros just to get its horn.

AMANDA: It is. And we can't get any more of it even if we wanted to.

JEFF: The rhinoceros is an endangered species, isn't it? I bet if you try to import rhino horn into the country these days, Greenpeace will be down on your necks.

TONY *(pointing to a glass jar)*: What are these yucky-looking lumps?

AMANDA *(reluctantly)*: Tiger gall. *(She adds quickly)* We don't sell much of that, either, because —

LEILA: Tigers are an endangered species. You know, it looks like most of your stuff is just for show.

KATHY *(trying to make up for LEILA's rudeness)*: What are in these little paper packages, Amanda? *(She holds up one of the wrapped packages AMANDA prepared earlier.)*

AMANDA: They're cough mixtures. We sell lots of them. So my parents always have a few batches ready. You steep the mixture in some hot water and drink it.

KATHY *(holding the package to her nose and sniffing)*: It smells a little like licorice.

AMANDA: The stuff in there that does most of the work is called coltsfoot.

LEILA *(giggling)*: Coltsfoot? Why not? You've got deer antler and rhino horn already. Sounds like, you know, a witch's brew.

JEFF *(promptly)*: "Eye of newt and toe of frog." *Macbeth*, Act Four, Scene One.

LEILA *(tiredly)*: English three, Section two. Jeff, we all took the course, you know. So you got an A in it. You don't have to remind us all the time.

KATHY *(quickly)*:   What is coltsfoot, Amanda? It's not really made from the foot of a colt, is it?

AMANDA: Coltsfoot is an herb. Maybe it's called that because the flower is shaped like the hoof of a young horse, or colt.

LEILA: What are we? Getting an extra-credit course on Chinese herbs?

AMANDA *(stiffly)*:   I thought you people came because you wanted to know about Chinese medicines.

LEILA: Herbs are for salads. I never heard of anyone curing a cold with, you know, a salad.

AMANDA: Herbs can be used for medicines, too. Chinese herbal medicines have been used for thousands of years. And they don't have funny side effects, either, because if they did, we'd know by now.

> TONY *is poking around the small heaps of herbs on the table. He picks up a dried root from one of the pieces of paper and holds it up.*

TONY: Hey, you guys! Doesn't this look just like a pair of human legs? I bet it's got supernatural powers!

He laughs. LEILA *goes up to him, takes the piece of root out of his hand, and looks at it. They whisper and nudge one another.* JEFF *joins them to have a look, but* LEILA *turns her back on him.*

JEFF *(turning back to* AMANDA*)*: Seriously, Amanda, isn't this herbal stuff mainly for health nuts? If you're *really* sick, you use modern medicines, right?

AMANDA *(coldly)*: Many of your modern drugs come from traditional herbal medicines, Jeff.

JEFF *(startled)*: Yeah, I guess you're right. Digitalis comes from foxglove. I forgot about that. And . . . let's see . . . the drug atropine comes from the deadly nightshade plant, doesn't it?

LEILA: Wow, another lecture from Professor Jeff Davidson.

TONY *(picking up a piece of herb from another heap and sniffing)*: Say, this one smells like grass!

AMANDA: It *is* a kind of grass.

TONY *(with a sly grin)*: I mean GRASS grass—pot— the kind you smoke.

AMANDA *(coldly)*: It's not pot. You'd better put it

down before you forget which pile you got it from. Otherwise the prescriptions will get mixed up.

LEILA: You mean you follow prescriptions? Like, you know, in a real drugstore?

AMANDA *(proudly)*: This *is* a real drugstore. Except that our drugs are all made from natural ingredients, not chemicals.

LEILA *(scornfully)*: I suppose when your customer hands you a prescription from his doctor, you fill it like in a pharmacy.

TONY *(chortling)*: Except that the prescription is written in Chinese! But it doesn't make any difference, because nobody can read the writing on a prescription anyway.

> An OLD CHINESE WOMAN *enters the store, looks nervously at the teenagers, then speaks quietly to* AMANDA *and hands her a slip of paper.* AMANDA *nods and, using her scoop and scales, proceeds to measure out quantities of medicine from various boxes and drawers onto a piece of paper. She stops to consult the prescription slip every now and then. Fascinated,*

JEFF, TONY, *and* KATHY *watch in silence. Finally* AMANDA *is finished. She folds up the paper around the mixture and does some rapid calculations on the abacus.*

AMANDA: That will be $2.35, please.

The OLD WOMAN *hands her some money, nods her head, and leaves the shop.*

KATHY: You really did it, Amanda! You really filled that woman's prescription, didn't you?

AMANDA *(proudly)*: I had to practice for five years before my parents trusted me to fill prescriptions.

JEFF: My uncle is a pharmacist, and he had to go to college and get a degree in pharmacy before he could fill prescriptions.

AMANDA: You do need a degree to fill chemical prescriptions. But I'm allowed to prepare the herbal medicines because they're much weaker than the chemical ones.

JEFF *(picking up one of the brass weights in the balance scales)*: Is this your basic unit of measurement? How much does it weigh?

AMANDA: It's about an ounce, maybe a little less.

JEFF: An ounce? That's a big amount! In my uncle's pharmacy, everything is measured in milligrams, which are ... let's see ... an ounce is about twenty-eight grams ...

LEILA *(muttering)*: There goes our great genius again, showing off.

AMANDA: I know you use much finer units in Western medicines, Jeff. That's why your pills are small, and our medicines come in heaps like these. But that doesn't mean I can be careless when I measure things out.

JEFF *(taking the set of scales from AMANDA and examining them)*: Say, these are neat! Maybe we can use them in our science class.

AMANDA *(anxiously)*: Be careful—the little brass weights are hard to replace.

JEFF *(Puts the heaviest weight into one of the pans of the balance. The scale tips suddenly, and all the weights are spilled. Several land on the floor.)*: Oops, sorry! *(He crawls under the table to pick up the weights, and when he stands up, he bumps his head against the table. The table shakes violently, and the piles of herbs become mixed up.)* Gosh, Amanda, I'm awfully sorry!

LEILA: Do you have to be such a klutz, Jeff?

JEFF: Aw, gee, I didn't mean to—

LEILA *(impatiently)*: Forget it. *(Turns to* TONY*)* Ready to go, Tony?

JEFF *(trying to keep* LEILA *and* TONY *from going)*: Speaking of witches, I hear they rub themselves all over with some kind of herb, and they get high— literally. They think they're flying on broomsticks. *(To* AMANDA*)* You got anything like that here?

AMANDA *(sighing)*: Can't you understand? We're not selling witches' brews here. We are a respectable medicine shop.

LEILA *(tired of the whole thing)*: Okay, so Amanda's herb shop is just a drugstore with, you know, a Chinese accent. Let's go. I've got loads of things to do. Coming, Tony?

TONY: All right, Leila. *(He looks once again at the piles of jumbled herbs on the table, and then grins at* AMANDA.*)* So Jeff was wrong about Chinese herbs. And I was all set to try something, too. *(He winks at* AMANDA, *flips a hand at* JEFF *and* KATHY, *then turns to leave with* LEILA *by the door on the left.* JEFF *starts to follow, but stops when he sees that* KATHY *is staying. He turns back reluctantly.)*

KATHY: You said your herbs aren't very strong, Amanda, but it *is* possible to overdose on Chinese drugs, isn't it? That opera singer who died here, for instance.

AMANDA *(defensively)*: The old man had a heart attack. We don't know that the medicine brought it on. Maybe his heart was already weak.

> KATHY *and* AMANDA *begin looking over the piles of herbs on the table to see if they can be salvaged.*

KATHY: Gee, I'm sorry, Amanda. I shouldn't have brought the others here. Can any of this be saved?

AMANDA *(sighing)*: I don't think so. They're too mixed up.

JEFF *(sheepishly)*: Did I tell you my parents went to court and legally changed my middle name to Butterfingers? *(He points at one pile.)* Hey, maybe you can still use this one. It doesn't look too bad.

AMANDA *(tightly)*: "Not too bad" is not good enough. How would you like it if you had strep throat, and your pharmacist uncle handed you a bottle of medicine that's "not too bad"?

KATHY: Look, Jeff, you've done enough already. You'd better leave well enough alone.

(KATHY helps AMANDA brush the piles of herbs together and throw the whole thing away in the wastebasket.)

JEFF: So an extra pinch of this and dash of that really make a difference, huh? Then these herbs can be pretty potent, after all.

AMANDA: Some of them are, like the one that old actor took. You can even overdose on ginseng, which most people think is a health tonic.

JEFF: No kidding? *(He becomes thoughtful.)* I bet you've got things here that can give people real hallucinations.

AMANDA: So you admit it! Except for Kathy, none of you ever paid any attention to me before. And now, all of you come into our store, even a big shot like Tony, because you think you can get a cheap thrill from some exotic Chinese drug.

JEFF: Well . . . *(Floundering a little, he brushes his hand against the abacus and sends it clattering to the floor and under the table.)* Oops, let me get it.

KATHY and AMANDA *(together)*: Don't move! I'll get it.

> *They both bend down quickly to pick up the abacus, and bump their heads. While* KATHY *winces and rubs her head,* AMANDA *gets up and puts the abacus on the counter, out of* JEFF'*s reach. After a second's thought, she also puts the scales away on the counter.*
>
> *Silently,* AMANDA *brings out more sheets of paper, spreads them out on the table, opens some drawers, and begins to measure out herbs with the scales.* JEFF *and* KATHY *stand watching her, and the silence becomes uncomfortable.* JEFF *goes to the counter and picks up the abacus.* KATHY *quickly takes it out of his hands and puts it down.*

KATHY: I'm sorry, Amanda. We've bothered you enough. I guess Jeff and I will be going. *(Pulling* JEFF *with her, she begins to walk toward the door leading to the street.)* See you in school tomorrow.

AMANDA: Wait, Kathy! *(She stops for a second, frowning. She turns to* JEFF.*)* What did you mean, getting a high from our Chinese drugs here? You mean like opium?

JEFF: Of course not! Gosh, you think I was saying there's an opium den in your basement?

KATHY: Jeff just thought that some of the drugs you have here can get you a little dopey, and make you see things. Look, let's forget about the whole thing. It's crazy, anyway.

AMANDA *(smiling suddenly)*: But it's not crazy at all. In fact we do have some drugs that can get you a little dopey. I know about mushrooms used by Mexican Indians. *(Pauses.)* Well, I may be able to come up with something—not as powerful, of course, but it might make you see a few things.

JEFF *(excited)*: Hey, I was right! So it wasn't a waste of time to come here after all!

KATHY *(alarmed)*: No, Jeff, we're not going to fool around with anything like that! It would be dangerous!

AMANDA: It's not dangerous. I wouldn't let him touch anything harmful, Kathy. If something bad happened, my parents would lose their license and even get into trouble with the police.

KATHY *(doubtfully)*: Well . . . but if your drug isn't powerful, it won't do much, either, will it?

AMANDA: Why don't you try some and see?

JEFF: Yeah! Come on, Kathy, let's try it! *(To* AMANDA*)* Do you have some right here?

AMANDA: No, I don't have anything ready prepared. I'd have to make up a batch. Why don't you come back later tonight, like after dinner?

JEFF *(delighted)*: That's great! And if it's as good as you say, we'll get Leila and Tony in on it, too!

KATHY *(still doubtful)*: I don't know, Jeff . . .

AMANDA: I promise that you won't come to any harm, Kathy.

JEFF: I knew you'd come through, Amanda! Come on, Kathy, let's go. We'll be back later tonight! *(They exit, with* KATHY *still shaking her head doubtfully.)*

AMANDA *(smiling as she watches them leave)*: I'll have to prepare something really special. I can't disappoint Jeff and Kathy, can I?

> *She starts rummaging around the drawers in the bureau, and takes out a cassette tape*

recorder. *She switches it on, and a high, wavering music is heard, scooping up and down in pitch. Though soft, it has a strangely shrill, piercing quality.*

As AMANDA *stands looking down at the cassette recorder, the door on the right opens and a figure glides silently into the room. It is dressed in a wide-sleeved tunic held together with a sash, and its trousers are tucked into soft boots. The figure is entirely in black, except for its face, which is covered with a dead-white mask. It weaves around slowly, dancing in time to the music. Then* AMANDA *clicks the cassette off, and in the silence the figure glides quietly out of the room.* AMANDA *has noticed nothing, and still stands looking down thoughtfully at the cassette recorder in her hands.*

SCENE 2

TIME: *Three hours later.*

AT CURTAIN'S RISE: *It is now dark, and the standing lamp has been lit. The table has been moved to one side of the room. On the counter is a small china bowl filled with a pungent ointment. Next to the bowl are several small pieces of oiled paper, round, and about the size of a half dollar.*

We hear the sound of a drawer closing. Then AMANDA *rises from behind the counter. She looks pleased with herself. She comes around to the front of the counter, goes over to the row of chairs, and moves them a bit until she has them arranged to her satisfaction. There is a knock on the door leading to the street.* AMANDA *goes to the door and opens it.*

AMANDA: Oh, hi. You're just in time. I've got everything ready. Come on in.

    JEFF *and* KATHY *enter.* JEFF *looks around eagerly, but* KATHY *is nervous.*

KATHY: I've been talking things over with Jeff, Amanda. I think we ought to call the whole thing off. If my parents find out I'm fooling around with Chinese drugs, they'll ground me for ten years and a day.

JEFF: Maybe *you* are ready to call the whole thing off, Kathy. I didn't say *I* was. Aw, come on. Amanda said Chinese drugs aren't so concentrated, remember? *(He notices the bowl and the pieces of oiled paper on the counter.)* Hey, is this the magic stuff that's going to do the trick?

AMANDA: Wait a minute, Jeff. *(She turns to KATHY.)* I don't want to go ahead with this unless both of you are quite sure you want to do it. If you don't feel good about this, Kathy, let's just forget it.

KATHY *(looking at JEFF, who is disappointed)*: Gee . . . I don't know . . . Well, first of all, what's in this stuff? Do we eat it, or what?

AMANDA *(holding up the bowl to KATHY)*: Here, smell it. What does it remind you of?

KATHY *(taking the bowl and sniffing at it gingerly)*: Mmm . . . *(Looks surprised.)* It doesn't smell that bad! I was expecting something awful, after you mentioned stuff like tiger gall and snakeskin.

JEFF *(eagerly taking the bowl and raising it to his nose)*: Hey, I know what this reminds me of: mint. *(He puts a dab of it on his tongue before KATHY can stop him. He hisses.)* Wow, it's hot! Do we have to eat a lot of it?

KATHY *(looking anxiously at JEFF)*: At least you're not rolling on the ground in agony.

JEFF: And I'm not turning into a hairy monster, either.

AMANDA: You really thought for a moment that I'd poison you, or turn you into a hairy monster? *(Beginning to sound angry)* Look, I'm not the one who started all this. Like I said, if you don't feel comfortable with it, we'll stop right here and go home. I've got a big set of math problems due tomorrow.

JEFF: Hey, I was only kidding, Amanda.

KATHY *(quickly)*: I'm sorry, Amanda, I didn't mean to hurt your feelings. But it's scary to swallow something mysterious like this without knowing what's going to happen.

AMANDA *(relenting)*: All right, I can't blame you for feeling nervous. Okay, first of all, you don't eat this stuff. It's an ointment. You put some on this scrap of oiled paper, and plaster it on your forehead. *(She demonstrates by placing one of the small round patches on the middle of her forehead.)* Like this, see.

JEFF: Will this work as well as something taken internally?

AMANDA: Why not? You're the one who mentioned witches rubbing stuff on their skin and getting high.

KATHY: I just remembered: My mom used to take a drug for seasickness, and instead of swallowing a pill, she rubbed something behind her ear.

JEFF (*slowly*): You're right. I guess it *is* possible to absorb something through your skin. In fact my uncle says people in the old days used to put mustard plasters on their chests for colds. How long will it take for your ointment to work, Amanda?

AMANDA: You may get a bit dizzy after a minute. So it's better if you stay seated. Your eyes will get heavy, and you'll start feeling sleepy. After that, you'll start to see things—maybe.

JEFF: What do you mean, maybe? I thought that's what we came here for.

AMANDA: Look, I don't make any promises, okay? To play safe, I'm not making the ointment very strong. So you might not see anything at all.

KATHY: Amanda is right, Jeff. It's better to be safe than sorry.

AMANDA *(looking from* JEFF *to* KATHY*)*: Well? What about it? Do you want to give it a try?

JEFF: Okay, I'm satisfied. Let's get going!

AMANDA *(turning to* KATHY*)*: How about you, Kathy? I'll give you the ointment only if you both agree to take it.

KATHY *(hesitating, but then making up her mind)*: Well, all right. I'm game.

> AMANDA *nods. She smears a generous dab of the ointment from the china bowl on each of two pieces of the oiled paper. She hands one to* JEFF *and one to* KATHY.

JEFF: Well, here goes. *(He puts the small round on his forehead, and can't resist crossing his eyes and making a face).* Come on, Kathy, now it's your turn. It doesn't hurt a bit. In fact it feels cool and rather pleasant.

> KATHY *sticks the patch on her head as well. She and* JEFF *look at each other, and they giggle self-consciously.*

KATHY: What happens now, Amanda?

JEFF *(eagerly)*: Yeah, when does the happy hour begin?

AMANDA: You'll have to be patient. Why don't you sit down and relax? It works better if you're relaxed.

> KATHY *quickly sits down on one of the wooden chairs, but* JEFF *prefers to walk around, looking at the glass jars on the shelves and fiddling with the pair of scales.* AMANDA *moves to a corner of the room and stands with her arms crossed. She watches the other two carefully. Suddenly* JEFF *drops the scales with a clatter.*

JEFF: Oops, Butterfingers at work again. Or maybe I'm getting a bit woozy. *(He walks over to* KATHY.*)* How do *you* feel, Kathy?

KATHY *(rubbing her eyes)*:   I feel hot. Maybe a little light-headed, too. Why don't you sit down, Jeff? You make me dizzy, moving around like that.

JEFF: Yeah, maybe I will. *(He flops down clumsily on the chair.)*

AMANDA *(in a hypnotically soothing voice)*:   Try to sit back and relax. . . . Your eyes are getting heavy. . . . You're feeling very sleepy. . . . Don't fight it. . . .

JEFF *(a little thickly)*:   Yes, ma'am, anything you say,

ma'am. *(He sits back and leans his head on* KATHY's *shoulder.)*

KATHY *(yawning)*: I think I'm falling asleep. You think I'm going to have a nice dream, Amanda?

AMANDA *(smiling)*: Sure you are. Isn't that what you came for?

JEFF *(muttering indistinctly)*: Make mine a nightmare. I want a really scary nightmare.

> AMANDA *drops down behind the counter and disappears from view. Suddenly the room becomes much darker. The only light comes from the right side of the stage, where the door leading to the back of the house has been left slightly ajar.*

AMANDA: I'm going to the kitchen to wash the bowl. I'll be right back. Will you be okay?

> KATHY *and* JEFF *mumble something. They seem to be only partially awake, and don't even notice when* AMANDA *leaves the room with the china bowl. She opens the door fully, and in the brighter light we see* KATHY *and* JEFF *leaning against each other on two chairs, with their heads drooping.* AMANDA *goes out the door*

and partially closes it again, leaving a slightly wider crack than before. There is the sound of a faucet being turned on, and a clatter of china. After the tap is turned off, there is a silence. JEFF murmurs something to KATHY, and she nods. Another longer silence follows. Suddenly the silence is broken by a high, wavering sound. JEFF moves sluggishly.

JEFF *(mumbling)*:   What's that?

KATHY *(raising her head with difficulty)*:   Hmmm?

The wavering sound is heard again, and at first it is like the strange music that AMANDA played earlier on the cassette tape. Then the music changes quality, as a falsetto voice begins to be heard. The crack in the door widens, and a figure advances into the room. The light is too dim for the figure to be seen clearly. There is an impression of a dead-white face, wearing a ferocious grimace. Dressed in a dark tunic held by a sash, and trousers tucked into soft boots, the figure is holding a long spear in its hands. It begins to step and turn in time to the music. A metallic crashing beat is heard in the background of the music, giving it rhythmic drive.

Soon the tempo accelerates. The spear swings faster and faster in the hands of the menacing figure. At one particularly wide swing, JEFF *shrinks back.*

JEFF: Yikes. That was close!

KATHY *(muttering)*: This is just a nightmare. . . .

The metallic clanging gets faster, and it is joined by a sound like two wooden sticks beating together. The tempo finally reaches a frantic climax. The figure stamps its feet faster and faster, until the music comes to a crashing close. With one hand holding up the spear, the figure stands motionless in the sudden silence. Before JEFF *and* KATHY *can move, the figure goes out. The door is closed, and the room becomes completely dark.*

KATHY *(desperately)*: Jeff, I've gone blind!

JEFF: Don't panic, Kathy! There's nothing wrong with your eyes!

KATHY: But I can't see!

JEFF: The lights have gone out, that's all.

KATHY *(raising her voice)*: Amanda! Where are you?

*The door opens, and in the light from the hall
we see Amanda come in, look around, and then
stoop down. Suddenly the room is brightly lit.*

AMANDA: I guess the lamp got unplugged. *(She stands
up and peers at* JEFF *and* KATHY.*)* Well, did you see
anything? *(When neither* JEFF *nor* KATHY *replies im-
mediately, she looks curiously from one to the other.)* If
it didn't work, we can try again tomorrow, and
I'll make the ointment slightly stronger.

JEFF *(taking a deep breath)*: Oh, it worked all right.
It sure did. Wait till you hear about the nightmare
I had! *(He pulls the patch off and furiously rubs his
forehead.)*

KATHY *(also pulling off the patch)*: I was hoping for a
nice dream, but I had a horrible nightmare too.

AMANDA: That's the trouble. We can't always control what we see. Some nightmares can drive you
mad.

KATHY *(shouting)*: Stop it, Amanda! *(*AMANDA *stares
at her in surprise, and* KATHY *puts her hands over her
eyes.)* I'm sorry. I'm a bit shaken. *(Trying to smile)*
Do you have a bathroom here? I'd like to wash
my face.

AMANDA *(concerned)*: Sure, Kathy, come on, I'll show you where it is. Gee, I'm sorry. Maybe that ointment wasn't such a good idea after all.

> AMANDA *and* KATHY *exit from the door on the right.*

JEFF *(Left to himself, gets up somewhat unsteadily.)*: Boy, I'm thirsty. I wonder if there's anything to drink around here. *(He pokes around the shop, looking curiously at the paper boxes on the counter. His elbow bumps into the abacus and sends it rolling. It falls down the other side of the counter.)*

JEFF: Uh-oh, there goes old Butterfingers again. *(He goes around to the other side of the counter and bends down. He is out of sight, but his voice can be heard.)* Where did that abacus roll to? There it is . . . ouch! Bumped my head against that open drawer. . . . Hey, what's this in the drawer?

> *The voices of* KATHY *and* AMANDA *are heard approaching.* JEFF *stands up and quickly moves in front of the counter and sits down. He begins to whistle thoughtfully.* KATHY *enters, followed by* AMANDA. KATHY *looks much better. She has washed her face and combed her hair, and she is even laughing a little.*

KATHY: . . . and then this hideous figure begins to stomp around, waving a long spear, or something. I could hear an awful noise the whole time, kind of like a strangled scream. But it had rhythm, too. It's crazy, but it was sort of like dancing.

> AMANDA *looks hard at* JEFF, *but when she sees him sitting quietly on the chair, she relaxes.*

JEFF *(looking curiously at* KATHY*)*: You saw a dark figure waving a spear around? That's funny! I saw exactly the same thing! *(Turning to* AMANDA*)* How can two people have the same hallucination?

AMANDA *(thoughtfully)*: I bet I can guess what happened. You remember that story I told you about the old opera singer who died right here in the shop? You must have been thinking about it subconsciously, and the drug made it all come out.

JEFF: What came out was a figure stomping around and waving a spear. What does that have to do with opera?

KATHY *(eagerly)*: I know! He was in *Chinese* opera. Wasn't he, Amanda?

AMANDA: That's right, he was. We still have a Chinese opera troupe here in Chinatown. . . .

KATHY: I saw a TV program about Chinese opera, and it was sort of like the figure in my nightmare. That must be it.

> JEFF *begins to pace back and forth silently, thinking deeply. Suddenly the silence is broken by a thread of sound.* JEFF, KATHY, *and* AMANDA *freeze in their places like statues. The sound, high, but with a strong pounding beat, is like the one heard earlier accompanying the eerie figure with the spear, only not so loud. Then it dies away gradually. The three teenagers come out of their frozen stances.* JEFF *resumes his pacing, glancing curiously at* AMANDA *occasionally.* KATHY *looks puzzled and cups her hand to her ear.*

KATHY: I thought I heard that funny music again, the one in my hallucination. It must be still the effect of the ointment. Is it going to last a long time?

AMANDA *(frowning and glancing quickly behind the counter)*: What? Uh . . . yes . . . that must be it. But I wouldn't worry. It'll wear off after about an hour.

JEFF *(stretching and yawning)*: Maybe we'd better be going, Kathy.

KATHY: Yes, it's getting late. I told my folks I came over to get help with my math homework. If I stay out much longer, they'll get suspicious.

AMANDA *(nodding)*: It is late, and I still have some problems left to do.

KATHY: Thanks a lot for everything, Amanda. But I sure got more than I bargained for.

JEFF: Yeah, thanks, Amanda. *(With emphasis)* You went to a lot of trouble. *(AMANDA stares suspiciously at JEFF, but he looks innocently back at her. JEFF starts to walk toward the left exit, and then stops and turns to AMANDA.)* I was wondering . . . you remember I said that if this herb thing works, maybe we could get Tony and Leila in on it, too.

KATHY: Oh, Jeff, we can't ask Amanda to go through all this again!

AMANDA *(smiling)*: That's all right. Bring Tony and Leila over tomorrow night, if they'll come. Leila'll think the whole thing is boring, though. She thinks almost everything is boring.

JEFF: After the experience we had tonight? She won't be bored!

KATHY *(still worried)*: But some of the herbs you used in the ointment might be expensive, Amanda. Won't you get into trouble with your parents when they see their supplies getting low?

AMANDA: Don't worry, I didn't use anything expensive that they'll miss. All right, why don't you bring the others here at the same time tomorrow night?

JEFF: Gee, thanks, Amanda. I won't forget this!

AMANDA: I'm sure you won't. (KATHY *stares at her curiously, but* AMANDA *only looks back blandly.*) Good night, Kathy.

> *Murmuring good-bye,* KATHY *and* JEFF *exit through the door on the left. The light goes out, and the stage becomes dark. After a while, a spotlight shines on* JEFF *and* KATHY, *who are standing at the bus stop outside the medicine store on the left apron of the stage. They are arguing.*

KATHY: I don't believe it! After she worked so hard to do us a favor!

JEFF: Oh, Amanda worked hard all right—not to do us a favor, but to have some fun at our expense. Look, the whole thing was a put-up job! The ointment, the weird music, the scary figure.

KATHY: What makes you think so?

JEFF: First of all, this figure with the spear that we both saw—remember I asked Amanda how the two of us could have the same hallucination? She said it was because we were both thinking about that Chinese opera singer who died in the shop.

KATHY: That makes sense. Chinese opera *does* have figures like that. I told you that I saw a TV program about it.

JEFF *(triumphantly)*: But the point is *I* never saw a TV program about Chinese opera, and I had no idea what it ought to look like. So how come I had the same hallucination?

KATHY *(staring)*: I guess you're right. *(After a pause)* Jeff, do you think we actually saw the ghost? *(She shivers.)* The ghost of the opera singer who's supposed to be haunting the shop?

JEFF: A ghost conjured up by drugs? First time I've heard of anything like that.

KATHY: Well, remember those witches rubbing themselves with herbs and getting hallucinations. Maybe that's how they conjured up supernatural spirits, too.

JEFF *(shaking his head)*: Come on, now you're telling me you really believe in ghosts and witches!

KATHY: I'm just keeping an open mind.

JEFF: Well, I'm not buying any of this. Besides, I have *proof* that Amanda was tricking us.

KATHY: What? What do you mean, Jeff?

JEFF: You know when you were in the bathroom with Amanda? Well, I was playing with the abacus, and I dropped it. When I went behind the counter to pick it up, I noticed that a drawer in the lower part of the bureau was open. *(Pausing for dramatic effect)* Guess what I saw in the drawer?

KATHY: Well? What?

JEFF: I saw a cassette tape player! *(KATHY stares, and JEFF grins triumphantly.)* Makes you think, doesn't it?

KATHY *(slowly)*: So that weird music—that falsetto

singing, and those crashing cymbals—they were all from some Chinese opera cassette tape!

JEFF: Right! A tape you can probably buy right here in Chinatown. And I'll bet you anything that Amanda herself was the figure with the spear.

KATHY: She did say they have an opera troupe here. She probably belongs to it.

JEFF: It'll be easy to check that out.

KATHY: But why should Amanda play such a trick on us? She's my friend!

JEFF: She may be *your* friend. But there's no reason why she's friends with the rest of us. Maybe she's sore at us for some reason.

KATHY *(thinking it over)*: Why shouldn't she be? She's a quiet kid, and none of you pay any attention to her in school. And then when you come to her parents' shop, you all sneer at everything, especially Leila.

JEFF: So—quiet little Amanda went to work and planned this whole thing.

KATHY: All right, Jeff, you've convinced me. We'd

better tell Amanda that we found out about the trick.

JEFF *(shaking his head)*:   No way! I've got a great idea for paying Amanda back.

KATHY *(firmly)*:   I don't want any part of it, Jeff.

JEFF *(indignantly)*:   Amanda made a fool out of me!

KATHY: But she *didn't* make a fool out of you. She didn't fool you after all.

JEFF: She must be laughing like mad right now, thinking about how we sat there like idiots, with those stupid patches on our foreheads!

KATHY *(grinning)*:   We did look like idiots, didn't we?

After a while, JEFF *begins to grin also.*

JEFF: Okay, Amanda pulled a good trick on us, and we deserved it. But I still want to get even with her. Don't you want to help me? You've always been such a good sport.

KATHY doesn't answer at first. Then she looks seriously at JEFF.

KATHY: I helped you before because I liked you, Jeff. You try too hard to be clever, and you're always clumsy, but I still liked you because you're kindhearted. Well, I'm not sure anymore that you're kindhearted. I'm not sure anymore that I even like you.

JEFF *blinks and stares at* KATHY *for a moment. Then he sticks his hands in his pockets and walks back and forth moodily, glancing every now and then at* KATHY. *Finally he stops and faces her.*

JEFF: Then what about Amanda? Do you call her kindhearted? After the trick she pulled on us?

KATHY: She only let us come to her shop in the first place because she wanted to do me a favor. But after we made all those nasty cracks about Chinese drugs, I don't blame her for wanting to play a trick on us. So let's call it quits now.

JEFF: Tony and Leila made most of the nasty cracks, not me. My scheme is going to make them the victims, too.

KATHY: I won't help you do anything that will hurt Amanda.

JEFF: It'll just be a joke, Kathy. And if Amanda can't take a little joke, do you still want her for a friend?

KATHY: Well . . . first tell me what your plan is.

JEFF: Here comes our bus. Look, I'll tell you my idea in school tomorrow. We can turn the tables on Amanda, and still make Tony and Leila the butts of the joke. But I'm going to need your help, Kathy.

SCENE 3

TIME: *One day later, about nine o'clock at night.*

AT CURTAIN'S RISE: *The wooden chairs are arranged a little differently; otherwise the set is the same as before.* AMANDA *enters from door on the right, carrying her cassette tape recorder in her hand. She sits down on one of the chairs and punches the button for rewind on the recorder. The tape whirs for a while, and then* AMANDA *pushes the stop button. She pushes the play button, and Chinese opera music is heard. She pushes fast forward and then back to play, and does this several times until she gets to the place she wants.*

AMANDA: There, that should do it. Funny, I wonder what made the machine suddenly go on and off by itself last night. *(She shrugs.)* Oh well, you never know with machines. It seems to be okay now.

She goes behind the counter and bends down out of sight. There is the sound of a drawer being pulled out. AMANDA *stands up and goes out by the door on the right. She returns with the china bowl of ointment and round pieces of oiled paper, which she places on the table. She is just in time. Voices are heard outside, and there is a knock on the door.* AMANDA *goes over to open it.* JEFF, KATHY, TONY, *and* LEILA *enter from left.*

TONY: Hi, Amanda. Heard you had a real blast here last night. Leila and I came to see for ourselves.

LEILA: Jeff kept on and on about seeing, you know, a weird figure waving a spear. Of course Tony had to come and check it out.

TONY *(winking)*: Can't let Jeff and Kathy have all the fun, can we?

LEILA: Jeff always exaggerates, Tony. You don't want to believe everything he says, you know.

JEFF: Kathy saw some things too, Leila.

LEILA (*shrugging*): Kathy—she always goes along with anything *you* say—we all know that.

KATHY (*protesting*): That's not true, Leila. (LEILA *rolls her eyes, but doesn't bother to answer.*)

JEFF (*slowly*): Kathy is a pretty decent kid. (*Turning to* KATHY) I was just too dumb to notice it before, Kathy.

TONY (*who has been nervous and restless*): Come on, everybody. We're wasting time standing around here talking. Let's get going. Okay, Amanda, what have you got for us? (*He goes over to inspect the china bowl on the table.*) Is this the famous magic ointment? (*He picks up the bowl and sniffs.*)

AMANDA (*taking the bowl from* TONY *and looking around*): Does this mean you are all going to try it?

KATHY: Just a minute, Amanda, before I forget: I think I left my comb in the bathroom last night. Can we go look for it?

AMANDA: Oh, all right.

> She puts the bowl down and accompanies KATHY *through the door on the right.* JEFF

knocks his hand against the abacus, sending it clattering to the other side of the counter. He goes around the counter quickly and drops down out of sight. A few seconds later he stands up, dusting his hands and looking very satisfied. TONY *glances curiously at him, but* LEILA *pays no attention. She flops down on one of the chairs.*

LEILA: This is so bo-o-ring. Do we have to go through with it?

JEFF: You won't be bored much longer. I, Jeff Davidson, guarantee it absolutely.

LEILA pouts at him, but before she can speak, AMANDA and KATHY return.

KATHY: That's funny. I was sure I left the comb here. Maybe it's at home after all.

AMANDA (*picking up the bowl and smearing the ointment on four pieces of oiled paper*): I wasn't sure about the dosage, but it seemed to work fine last night, so I'm making it the same strength tonight. (*She wipes the excess ointment from her hands.*) Here you go.

JEFF *and* KATHY *take their patches and im-mediately apply them to their foreheads. After a moment,* LEILA *gets up languidly from her chair, picks up a patch, and puts it on.* TONY *is still hanging back.*

JEFF: What's the matter, Tony? Scared? You're the one who sounded so impatient a minute ago. Or was that just talk?

TONY *(quickly)*: I'm not scared! *(Hesitating)* Uh . . . how did you feel today, Jeff? Not sluggish or anything?

JEFF: I felt great all day! No aftereffects. What are you afraid of?

TONY: I can't afford to get sluggish—the team has an important practice tomorrow.

AMANDA: I don't believe in forcing anybody into anything. If you're unhappy about this, Tony, for-get about the ointment and go right on home. We understand.

JEFF: Yeah, we understand, all right.

TONY *(shrugging)*: Oh, well, what the heck! *(He picks up the remaining patch and sticks it on. He looks around at the others.)* What happens next?

JEFF *(like an old hand)*: What happens next is we all sit down and wait.

KATHY: Yes, it's a good idea to sit down, because you'll get a little dizzy in a minute.

LEILA *(putting a hand to her head)*: Ooh . . . I feel dizzy already.

> *She quickly sits back down on her chair.* TONY *sits down carefully beside her. When he thinks no one is looking, he takes his own pulse.* KATHY *and* JEFF *sit on the remaining chairs.*

AMANDA: Make yourselves comfortable. In a minute you'll start feeling a bit sleepy, but don't let it bother you. I'll be back as soon as I rinse off this bowl.

> AMANDA *picks up the bowl and, after taking a look at her four schoolmates, goes out the door on the right.* JEFF *and* KATHY *whisper to each other.* LEILA *tries to talk to* TONY, *but he is busy taking his pulse. After a while* LEILA's *head droops.*

LEILA *(muttering)*: Bo-o-ring.

TONY *(murmuring indistinctly)*: Take it easy, Leila.

Again, as on the previous night, the room suddenly turns darker, and the only light is from the crack in the door. JEFF *sits up and pokes* KATHY. *Then the silence is broken by the same quavering sound as on the previous night, only this time it is softer.* JEFF *and* KATHY *stare at each other in astonishment.*

KATHY *(whispering)*: So you didn't change the tape after all. I thought I gave you lots of time.

JEFF: I don't understand! I thought I did change the tape. Maybe I was in a hurry, and put Amanda's original tape back in by mistake. . . .

His voice peters out. The door on the right is opening wider, and once more the eerie figure glides in. To the time of the high, rhythmic music, it begins to weave around the room, waving the spear. TONY *raises his head and stares.* LEILA *stirs, noticing the nightmarish figure for the first time, and whimpers.*

TONY *(muttering)*: Jeez, that ointment must be powerful stuff!

LEILA *(moaning)*: I'm scared, Tony!

Suddenly the Chinese opera music is replaced by a crash of loud rock music, with a thumping bass. The heads of all four teenagers jerk up. The figure with the spear stops its weaving motion as the music washes over the room. Then the spear twirls again, and the figure resumes its dance. But the dance this time is different. The figure twists and whirls and bends and stamps, throwing itself violently into the rock beat. JEFF *jumps up and starts to laugh. Soon* JEFF *and* KATHY *begin to clap their hands in time to the music.* TONY *and* LEILA *sit stunned in their chairs. Then* JEFF *gropes his way behind the counter. There is a click, and the music stops. He moves next to the plug of the standing lamp. After a moment, the light suddenly goes on in the room. The fantastical figure now stands motionless, with one hand on its hip and the other one resting the spear on the ground. In the bright light, the figure looks no longer nightmarish, only outlandish. The white face, painted with a red mouth and horizontal streaks of black, is shown to be a mask.*

TONY *(blinking)*: Wha' . . . what . . . will somebody tell me what's going on?

LEILA *(shrieking)*: The ghost! We're seeing the ghost of that Chinese opera singer!

> JEFF *and* KATHY *burst out laughing again. Then the figure with the spear raises the mask, uncovering the face of* AMANDA. *For an instant she stands with her lips trembling. Then she bursts out laughing as well.* JEFF, KATHY, *and* AMANDA *are almost doubled over with laughter, with* JEFF *slapping his thigh,* KATHY *wiping her eyes with the back of her hand, and* AMANDA *pounding the butt of the spear on the ground.*

LEILA *(finally understanding)*: It's a dirty trick! *(Furiously tearing off the round patch from her head)* Jeff Davidson, you planned the whole thing! You tricked me! *(Turning to* TONY*)* Take me home this instant!

> But TONY *is not listening to her. His shoulders are quivering, and suddenly a loud hoot breaks from him. He removes the patch from his forehead, stares at it, and joins the others in laughter.*

TONY *(when he is able to speak again)*: I didn't know you had it in you, Jeff. When you were talking about that powerful stuff you took—the dizziness and everything—you really had me fooled!

LEILA *(even angrier)*: And Kathy was in on it too! *(Snarling at* KATHY*)* You and your precious friend Amanda set this up! I know you're jealous of me, so you're doing this to make me look stupid!

TONY *(still laughing)*: Okay, whose idea was it? The three of you worked together, didn't you? And you staged that scene here yesterday afternoon.

KATHY *(puzzled)*: What do you mean, Tony? Staged what scene here?

TONY: When you mentioned that scary story of the Chinese opera singer who died in this room. It certainly put us into the right mood for Amanda's act.

AMANDA *(slowly)*: We didn't work together at all. In fact I pulled the same trick on Jeff and Kathy last night—gave them the ointment, and did my Chinese opera act.

JEFF: What was really in the ointment, Amanda? It had a minty smell, but you made up the bit about hallucinations, didn't you?

AMANDA *(laughing)*: What I used was something

called Tiger Balm, an ointment you rub on your temples for relieving headaches and neuralgia. My grandmother and some of her friends swear by it.

JEFF: What gives the ointment that cool sensation we felt?

AMANDA: Oil of peppermint, probably. Personally, I think the ointment is mainly Vaseline, with some spices and perfumes added to give it an exotic smell.

KATHY: Is it also a sedative? Was that why we felt sleepy at first?

AMANDA: You felt sleepy because I told you that you were sleepy. *(She laughs.)* It's amazing how powerful suggestion can be.

LEILA *(yawning conspicuously)*: Well, your suggestion is certainly working. I'm falling asleep, you know, on my feet. Tony, take me home.

TONY *(looking at* AMANDA*)*: So Jeff was wrong. We can't get any hallucinations on any of the herbs in your store, can we?

AMANDA: To tell the truth, I don't even know. I

have much better things to do. Anyway, since I'm in the opera troupe, I can't afford to take anything that'll spoil my timing.

TONY: Hey, that's right. That dance you did with the spear is kind of like acrobatics.

AMANDA *(proudly)*: Chinese opera performers have to train like athletes. So I don't fool around with anything that messes up my coordination.

TONY *(looking suddenly cheerful)*: Absolutely! You know, I'll have to tell that to the other guys next time they lean on me.

KATHY: Was that tape something used by your Chinese opera troupe, Amanda?

AMANDA *(nodding)*: It's one of the pieces we're rehearsing. Our troupe is also doing another one right now.

JEFF: What made that spooky, gliding sound? It was some sort of singing, but no human voice I ever heard makes that kind of noise.

AMANDA: I know what you mean. That spooky sound, as you call it, is made by a man's voice singing falsetto, accompanied by a Chinese violin and a bamboo flute playing in unison.

JEFF: What about that crashing beat? They sounded like a pile of pots and pans falling down.

AMANDA *(giggling)*: They did sound like pots and pans, didn't they? They were brass cymbals, and they're always used during battle scenes, which was what I did last night. Tonight's piece was going to be *The Dance of the Willow Spirit.* It was the favorite role of that old actor who died here in this shop.

LEILA *(shuddering)*:   You know, I wish you'd stop talking about that old man. It gives me the creeps.

AMANDA *(ignoring* LEILA *and looking curiously at* JEFF*)*: You must have found out I was playing a tape. How did you guess?

JEFF: I saw the open drawer behind the counter, and found the cassette tape recorder inside.

AMANDA *(smiling ruefully)*:   So you erased part of my Chinese opera tape, and put in rock music. How did you manage to do that?

JEFF *(baffled)*:   I didn't. I didn't have time. While you and Kathy went to the bathroom to look for her comb, I took out your cassette and put in my own tape with the rock music. I barely had time to put the machine in the drawer before you came back.

AMANDA *(bewildered)*: But . . . but . . . the tape started tonight with the Chinese opera section, and I even did some of my dance to the music. It didn't change into rock until later!

JEFF *(stuttering)*: M-my tape had nothing b-but rock on it. Where did the Chinese opera music come from?

> Stunned, AMANDA, JEFF, *and* KATHY *stare at one another.*

TONY *(not understanding what they are talking about, goes behind the counter and brings out the tape recorder. He pushes a button, and rock music starts again.)*: Come on, Amanda. Show me the routine with the spear.

> *He takes* AMANDA's *hand and pulls her into the middle of the room. At first she is too dazed to move. But soon she responds to the music, and she begins to do her dance with the spear in time to the rock beat.* TONY *watches her*

carefully, beating time to the music, and he is soon able to match her movements.

TONY: You really had me fooled, Amanda. You look like such a quiet girl in school, always doing the homework and everything. And all this time you're laughing at us behind our backs!

AMANDA: Keep dancing, Tony. I like you better with your mouth shut.

JEFF and KATHY watch the dancing for a while. Then JEFF makes an elaborate bow to KATHY and takes her by the hand to join the dancing. LEILA still sits on her chair, bored and nearly falling asleep.

Suddenly the rock music stops and changes back to the Chinese opera music. AMANDA, TONY, JEFF, and KATHY freeze in their places. The door to the right opens farther, and a figure in black with a dead-white face glides into the room. It is the one seen earlier behind AMANDA's back when she first played her opera tape. The figure moves behind the counter and begins to dance in time to the music.

Abruptly, the music changes back to rock, and the four young people resume their dancing.

Not once do they glance at the figure behind
their backs, which is also moving in time to the
rock beat.

CURTAIN

LENSEY NAMIOKA

Lensey Namioka was born in Beijing, China, but many of her novels for young people take place in feudal Japan, inspired by the history of her husband's family. She and her husband, a college math professor who was raised in the castle town of Himeji, Japan, have traveled all over the world and now reside in Seattle, Washington. Her experiences have also provided background for two travel books she has written on Japan and China.

Two young samurai warriors are Namioka's main characters in *White Serpent Castle*, where they struggle to unravel the mystery of the serpent-shaped castle. Their adventures continue in *The Samurai and the Long-Nosed Devils*, *Valley of the Cherry Trees*, *Village of the Vampire Cat*, and *Island of Ogres*. She is currently working on the sixth novel in that series, called *The Coming of the Bear*, which is set in Hokkaido and involves the Ainu, an aboriginal people.

In addition, Lensey Namioka has published *Who's Hu?*, a humorous story about a Chinese teenager, and a mystery-suspense novel, *Phantom of Tiger Mountain*, which takes place in China before the Mongol invasion.

Herbal Nightmare is Namioka's first published play. Her only previous dramatic work, she says, was a traumatic experience that occurred when she was in the eighth grade at the Peabody School in Cambridge, Massachusetts. In the musical version of Dickens's *A Christmas Carol*, she was cast as one of the Cratchet twins. When Bob Cratchet announced, "Here come the twins!" and she pranced onstage, hand in hand with a blond, blue-eyed boy, she recalls, "The audience broke up laughing, and I never trod the boards again."

Riding Out the Storm

by Cin Forshay-Lunsford

CHARACTERS

MICHAEL REDHAWK

KEITH: Michael's brother

DELORES: Michael's sister

BRIAN: Michael's friend

BONNIE: Michael's girlfriend

SERENA: Michael's friend

PAINTER: Michael's friend

SETTING

A vacant lot. The backdrop is a crumbling wall splattered with vibrant graffiti. This graffiti includes: the logos of popular rock bands, a peace sign, the anarchy symbol, a skull and crossbones, the infinity symbol, the yin/yang symbol, a large spray-painted heart inscribed "Michael and Bonnie," a cartoon cat, and several slogans such as "End Apartheid," "Kilroy Was Here," "The End Is Near," "Rock and Roll," "The World Rots," and "Truth Is Beauty." A few scraggly ivy vines creep over the top of the wall, and wildflowers bloom from a crack at its base. A section of the wall stage right should be left blank to accommodate PAINTER's *phoenix mural. It is suggested that the design be sketched lightly in pencil and color coded for the convenience of the actor playing the role of* PAINTER. *If this player is artistically inclined, he may wish to attempt the mural freehand, but it is cautioned that the time element should be kept in mind. The phoenix mural may be completed in spray paint or liquid paints, whichever the player prefers.*

A discarded bus seat, stuffing spilling from rips in its hide, has been pushed back close to the wall. Two crates on either side of the bus seat serve as chairs. The ground is littered with newspaper, cigarette packs, soda cans, and beer bottles. Ideally, the stage should be equipped with a forestage projecting a few feet from the proscenium. If this is not possible, a downstage center area may be set apart by creative lighting. This is the area where, at all points in the play involving flashbacks to scenes with MICHAEL, *the players will act out their parts. At those points in the play, the other characters freeze, and lights dim on them, creating the illusion of suspended time. An added element of nostalgia would be acquired through the use of a fog machine during the flashback sequences.*

As the curtain rises, PAINTER *is seen sitting dejectedly, cross-legged on the bus seat. His head is in his hands. He is a small, thin boy of fourteen who hides beneath a cap too large for him. It is obvious that something has upset him greatly.* SERENA *rushes onstage and stops abruptly when she sees him. She hesitates, as if frightened by the very question she is about to ask.* PAINTER *is deaf, and so* SERENA *signs to him as she speaks her lines.*

The time is the present.

SERENA: Painter! *(Moving closer to sit at his side)* Painter, I just heard something . . . something terrible. *(Studying his face)* It's true then. *(*PAINTER *nods and bites his lip, signing to her that* MICHAEL *is in the hospital.)* Oh God! I can't believe it. *(*KEITH *and* DELORES *enter stage right.* SERENA *rises and crosses the stage to meet them. She hugs* DELORES *and touches* KEITH'*s arm.)* I saw Bonnie at school. She was hysterical. She told me Michael got hurt. I tried to make her come with me, but she just wandered away from the lockers with her books pressed against her, and this wild look in her eyes.

KEITH: There was an accident last night. Mike lost control of his motorcycle, out on Snake Road. He couldn't make the turn, the one at the top of the hill. He . . . he hit the guardrail. He was thrown over the edge.

SERENA: Oh, Keith!

KEITH: Serena, he's bad. They don't know if he's going to make it. *(Trying to choke down the emotion in his voice)* Both of his legs were crushed, and he's bleeding inside.

DELORES: We went to the hospital. They won't even

let us see our brother. They won't tell us anything! I'm so scared!

KEITH: We waited around forever. It was too depressing. We just couldn't take that place anymore. He's still in surgery. The nurse says they won't be able to tell us anything more till that's over.

SERENA: How long will that take?

KEITH: Who knows? An hour, two, maybe more.

DELORES: What I don't understand is that the nurse said they brought him in at four this morning. It was raining so terribly hard then. What was he doing out on Snake Road at four in the morning in a colossal thunderstorm? It was sheer lunacy to attempt that curve on a bike, in the rain, in the dark.

KEITH: I don't get it either.

> BRIAN *pops his head over the top of the wall, smiles, nods, and lithely scrambles over. He is a burly, handsome, somewhat swaggering young man of sixteen. He is rather boisterous in a charming, disarming way. Brian is dressed in*

*jeans, boots, and a black muscle T-shirt, and
sports a rather sinister tattoo.*

BRIAN: What's up? *(It is evident that he knows nothing
about Michael's situation.)* How's it going, guys? Seen
Mikey around lately? He was supposed to meet
me at the overpass this morning, and the little
creep never showed.

DELORES: You haven't heard? It's all over the school.

BRIAN: I haven't been to school. Waiting around for
Mikey made me so late for class that I figured it
wasn't worth showing up for the last couple of
minutes. Write a note for me, would you, Delores?
*(BRIAN rips a sheet of looseleaf paper from his binder
and pulls a pen from his back pocket.)* You've got nice
handwriting. Here, write: "To Whom It May
Concern, Please excuse my son Brian's taaa-rrr-
diness. An important family matter needed his
attention." That sounds legit, don't you think?
And sign it "Sincerely, Mrs. Carol Burr." I figure
that sounds more general. Last month I had strep
throat, a stomach virus, pinkeye, mono, and my
grandmother died twice. I got busted for granny
kicking the bucket though; Vice Principal Leash
called to ask how I was taking the tragedy, and

my grandmother answered the phone. *(DELORES makes no move to write the note.)* Hey, what is with you guys? Where's the funeral, Longface? *(BRIAN cuffs* KEITH *playfully.* KEITH *shrugs him off.)* Hey! Hey! What is it? What's being said around school grounds that I haven't heard yet? *(The silence drags.)* Where's Mike? *(Beginning to panic)* I said where's Mikey? What's happened to my bud?

> BONNIE *enters stage left. She is a very pretty young girl, but she appears extremely disheveled and a little disoriented. There is a dazed look in her eyes as she shuffles across stage to collapse in a corner of the makeshift sofa. She has been crying, as witnessed by her smudged eye makeup, but now she appears to have passed that point. She speaks in a dull, raspy, nearly emotionless voice.*

BONNIE: He's dying. Michael's dying in the hospital and I can't save him.

DELORES: Stop it, Bonnie, don't talk like that. Michael's not going to die. I know my brother. He'll fight. He isn't a coward. He'll fight—

BONNIE: To the bitter end? *(BONNIE finishes DELORES'S sentence for her and laughs without mirth. To BRIAN)*

Michael tried to kill himself last night and screwed up. He's at the hospital. All twisted and broken.

BRIAN: What are you talking about? Are you nuts?

KEITH *(agitated)*: My baby brother *did not* try to kill himself! It was an accident; a stupid, unfortunate accident!

BONNIE: Can you be so sure?

KEITH: I don't ever want to hear you say a thing like that again.

BONNIE: Don't try to bully me.

BRIAN: What happened? How did Mike end up in the hospital?

DELORES: He went down on his bike. *(Passionately)* But he's *not* going to die. They have five different doctors working on his case. He's been in surgery for nearly four hours. He's holding his own, Bri. If he made it through the first part of the operation, he can make it through the last.

BRIAN *(enraged)*: Damn it, Mikey! Damn it! Why couldn't you have been more careful? Damn me! Why wasn't I with you? You shouldn't have been out there alone.

KEITH *(standing over* BONNIE *almost menacingly)*: Why did you say that about Michael? Bonnie, what made you tell that lie?

SERENA: Just leave her be. She's all upset, in shock or something. I don't think she means what she says. *(Rummaging in her pocketbook for a handkerchief and mirror,* SERENA *hands these items to* BONNIE.*)* Here, fix yourself up.

KEITH: Listen, Bonnie, I don't want to hear you ever saying shit like that about my brother again. I mean it. I don't know who you think you are, but if you think Mike's accident was anything *but* an accident, you're not the fine soulmate Michael liked to pretend you are.

BONNIE: Yeah, well maybe you're not the cherished, enlightened brother *you* like to pretend you are.

KEITH: What's that supposed to mean?

BONNIE: Michael was complex.

KEITH: Don't you dare speak of my brother in the past tense.

BONNIE: I'll dare what I will.

DELORES: Stop it, you two! Bickering like this won't help anything.

BRIAN: How bad is he?

KEITH *(pulling himself together)*: Both of his legs were badly crushed. One rib was broken and there's some internal bleeding. He hasn't regained consciousness. Perhaps for now that's for the best. The pain would be excruciating.

BRIAN: It's that bad?

BONNIE: It's worse.

KEITH: Meaning?

BONNIE: His spirit was wounded long ago, and no amount of love from me has been able to bind that hurt.

BRIAN *(pained by the question)*: Will he die?

KEITH: What kind of stupid-ass question is that?! Of course he's not gonna die. He's a kid. He can't just die.

BONNIE: Once I dreamed I died. I was dressed in this beautiful snowy-laced gown, laid out like some wax-perfect Juliet Capulet. Everyone came to the funeral, and they all wept and wrung their hands and said what a good kid I was and how much they were gonna miss me. My father came and told everybody that his very heart was broken in two because he never told me he loved me, and now I'd never know. In real life he always told me I was a worthless piece of shit and a bitch just like my mother, but in dreams that doesn't count. And my mother came and begged me to come back to her because she didn't want to be alone. Somehow, that didn't seem a good enough reason, so I insisted on remaining dead.

Tiny silver spiders came and spun me a gossamer shroud. It glittered in the moonglow as the pallbearers carried my body to the cemetery gate. You all came and sprinkled the bier with gemstones and creamy-pink seashells and the tenderest of rose blossoms. These shriveled, malevolent creatures, looking like something out of *Tales from the Crypt,* were lowering me into the hole in the ground and suddenly I freaked, thinking about those thin white worms, and the unnameable creatures that lurk in the thick of grave mire, and in the muck of a guilty mind.

The bearers lowered me down . . . down . . . I wanted to claw my way out of the grave, cursing and sputtering with indignation, but I couldn't move a muscle. I screamed inside my mind. The rope snapped. The bier plunged down. I was about to hit bottom when I caught myself and fell back into my body, back into my own bed . . . my own safe bed, musical Pooh Bear tucked beneath the coverlet.

DELORES: Make her stop talking like that!

SERENA: Really, Bonnie, chill out. We all feel bad, but you're only making it worse.

BONNIE: How can it be any worse?

BRIAN: What do you think happens to you when you die?

KEITH: Do we really have to talk about this?

BRIAN: I mean, you think that's the end? Like a flame snuffed out, we just disappear? When my father was still around, he used to take me and my little stepsister to the lake to go boating. Once Amy saw a dead dog lying on the side of the road. She started crying about how we should stop the car and get out and bury the thing. My dad told her the crows needed something to eat. That really set her off. Maybe it wasn't the best thing in the world to tell a four-year-old, but I understood his point. I mean, the life was gone from the dog. In my mind I saw it die: I even imagined that I was that little dog loping across the highway. There was a scent of danger; my muscles stiffened beneath the fur. Truck lights pierced the night, mesmerizing lights . . . and I cringed at the quick blast of a horn. One dangling moment of raw terror and confusion . . . and then the sudden, sickening, inevitable impact.

After: nothing. It would just end. I'd feel no pain, no pleasure. It would be as if I'd never been born. What use is there in pitying the dead? Or in pretending they live on somehow, somewhere, after dying?

When my father died, he died real slow. His illness made him sick for a long time before the end. He died from the inside out; tubes in his body, and a machine to prove some part of him was still alive because you couldn't tell otherwise. I think if it had been me, I wouldn't have died that way. If I knew, like he did, that certain death was only a matter of time, I'd put a bullet in my brain.

SERENA: That's the coward's way out. It takes more courage to live than it does to die.

BRIAN: That may be true, but I'll chose to die with dignity, when I can no longer live with dignity.

There was such anguish in my father's eyes, such shame. I would have helped him go myself, but I was even more of a coward. I loved him too much. I just couldn't do it, though I believe now he might have wanted me to. He was such a great big bear of a man even death couldn't strike him down in one blow; it took a million thrusts to kill him.

DELORES: I can't believe that death is the ultimate end. Maybe the soul in death breaks the barrier of an earthbound body to fly free. Sometimes in my happiest dreams I can fly and it feels so real, like I'm remembering how to do the simplest thing in the world. But I don't want to talk about dying. I can feel in my heart that my brother's going to survive this.

BRIAN: But what happens if—and I'm hoping, I swear, that it doesn't—Michael lives, but he ends up crippled, or brain damaged. You think Mikey would want to live an imperfect life?

SERENA: You cruel, unthinking brute! (PAINTER *has shied away from the group and is off in a corner to himself. Shutting out the others, he begins to paint something on the wall.)* What's wrong with you?

You know how self-conscious Painter is about his deafness. Even with us, he feels he's too different. Then you go and say something stupid like that. He *can* read lips, you know! He's one of the kindest, most talented people I've ever met. Don't you think he's been made to feel that his is an imperfect life? Just because *you* wouldn't want to struggle with a handicap doesn't mean a person faced with that challenge couldn't rise to the occasion. I pray Michael lives, and I pray that his legs heal and that he'll be able to walk again. But if it happens that he can never walk again, I'll still care, and I'll be as much of a friend as I ever was, if not more. Because if that happens, he'll need us that much more.

BRIAN: And what if he's suffered brain damage? Would he want to be trapped in a man's body with a child's mind? Would Mike ever let himself be spoon-fed; would he ever consent to someone helping him to go to the bathroom? No! Not if he could help it. That's all I'm saying. *(Crossing to* PAINTER*)* Listen, pal, you know I didn't mean anything by it. I wasn't trying to hurt you or anything. I think you're okay. I wasn't talking about being just deaf and mute, like you. I was talking about the possibility of severe paralysis. You know what an active, physical dude Mikey is. Can you imagine how he'd feel not being able to walk down the street with his arm around his girl? No longer able to ride his motorcycle? He'd go nuts!

PAINTER (PAINTER's *speech is slow and imperfect. It is as if each word were torn from inside him with great pain.*): I'm not mute, Brian. I've been deaf since birth, but I can speak. I know when I talk it sounds funny to people, so I'd rather not talk than talk and be laughed at.

SERENA *(shocked)*: Oh, Painter!

PAINTER: Serena says it's silly to hide this way, and maybe she is right. But it hurts, being different *(His voice cracks.)* when the world is slow to understand that different doesn't mean inferior.

BRIAN *(defensively)*: I'm sorry if what I said about Michael made you think I meant anything bad about you. I really didn't. *(Laughs.)* Christ, you can talk! You dog! Letting us think you couldn't!

SERENA: Becoming a part of the immersion program was Painter's parents' idea, not his own. Before he came to school here, he went to a school where all the students were deaf.

PAINTER: My paintings speak for me because it is hard for me to speak for myself. I may live an imperfect life, but I strive to create perfect art.

BRIAN (to SERENA): Show me how to say "Forgive me."

> SERENA shows him how to sign the message. BRIAN signs to PAINTER. PAINTER nods and returns to his work.

KEITH: If only there were some way to go back in time. I could stop him from riding. I feel like I should have done something.

DELORES: What could you have done? You had no way of knowing what was going to happen. None of us did. I didn't even know he left the house. Did you?

KEITH (shaking his head): He never said good-bye.

DELORES: Do you remember last Fourth of July, Keith? (Lights fade on the other characters. The projected stage is strangely illuminated, giving it an underwater quality. KEITH and DELORES step forward to *share the arena while the remaining characters freeze, save for* PAINTER, *who continues his work on the mural.)* It was such a gorgeous night, warm, balmy breeze blowing and that sweet smell of honeysuckle all about.

KEITH: We went up to the bluff to watch the fireworks. I'd just gotten my license.

> *The sound of crickets chirping fills the stage, punctuated by the whizz and pop of exploding bottle rockets.* DELORES *and* KEITH *point at the "night sky" over the audience's heads, oohing and aahing. On the ideal stage, a car fender prop would be lowered at the edge of the proscenium.* MICHAEL, *seen for the first time, enters stage left and walks center to lean up against the car fender.* DELORES *and* KEITH *have their backs to him, watching the fireworks display. A few strains of music herald his arrival—an exerpt from "Moonlight Drive" by The Doors.* MICHAEL *is compact and lively, with a quick, roguish laugh and self-assured air. He wears his dark hair stylishly long and likes adornments: an earring, silver skull rings, scarves, and chains around his motorcycle boots.*

MICHAEL: Wow! Did you see that one? The purple and red and gold? Man, that was somethin'. *(Sips from a bottle.)* Independence Day. It's got a nice ring to it. Hey, tell you what, Keith. What say we go fishing this weekend? We haven't done that in a long time. Saturday sound good?

DELORES: Oh, I wish you wouldn't! I feel so bad. How can you stand those poor things staring at you with their dead fishy eyes? It's cruel to kill them.

KEITH: Are you going to stay a vegetarian all your life? You're such a weirdo. Most veggies at least eat fish and eggs.

DELORES: I believe in animism.

MICHAEL: Oh, no! Dee's been sneaking peeks into the Webster's again.

KEITH: So what's animism?

DELORES: The belief that all natural creatures are endowed with a soul.

MICHAEL: You think that's for real?

DELORES: It bothers me to think of my brothers taking the life of anything that bleeds.

MICHAEL: You're too sensitive. You'd better toughen up if you want to make it in this world. So what do you say, bro?

KEITH: I can't go, Mike. I'm sorry.

MICHAEL: How come?

KEITH: Dad and I got plans. We're playing together in the softball tournament.

MICHAEL *(slightly sarcastic)*: Good luck.

KEITH: Why don't you come down and watch? You never come to our games.

MICHAEL: Yeah, well . . . no offense, but I've got a lot better things to do with my time than watch a bunch of stupid jocks swing a wooden stick and run around in circles.

KEITH: Oh come on, Michael. Don't start. Don't try to make me feel guilty because I get along okay with Dad and you don't lately.

MICHAEL: Lately? Are you joking? When did he ever have a single kind word for me?

KEITH: You're kind of hard on him too, you know. He's only human. The guy makes mistakes, but he tries.

MICHAEL: Maybe to you.

KEITH: Look, we'll go fishing next weekend instead, okay?

MICHAEL: What makes you think I still want to go with you? Don't do me any favors, brother.

KEITH: Mike, you're being ridiculous.

MICHAEL: Oh, shut up already.

KEITH: Why are you like this?

MICHAEL: Why the hell do you think?

KEITH: Because you're jealous.

MICHAEL: What do I have to be jealous about? If you want to waste your time with him, go ahead. Fine! See if I care.

DELORES: Cut it out, both of you.

MICHAEL: He always liked you better than me, but you think I give a shit? I don't. Not anymore.

KEITH: Oh bull! He loves us just the same.

MICHAEL: Oh yeah? Then how come you're "Son," and "Sport," and "Pal," and I'm "Hey, Stupid," and "You Bastard," and "Boy"?

KEITH: You never cut the guy any slack, Mike. You think it doesn't make Dad bitter when you act like you despise him?

MICHAEL: And how am I supposed to act, huh? Can you tell me that? Is it supposed to not bother me that you, his first-born son, his namesake, get all the attention and I get diddly-squat? I get blamed for everything that goes wrong. You take a shit and the world applauds.

KEITH: What about Mom, smart ass? Are you going to try and deny that you're her sweet baby boy? Her best-beloved and favorite son?

MICHAEL: Get real.

KEITH: Well, it's true, right?

MICHAEL: You're looney tunes.

KEITH: I remember the day they brought you home from the hospital. I was real little, but I still remember. No one wanted to know from me. They all rushed right past me to get to you. *(Mimicking)* "Oh look at that precious smile, everyone! Isn't he a treasure?" "He's so tiny and perfect! Just look at those itsy-bitsy fingernails." Even Uncle Harold, cool old Uncle Harold, who always had butterscotch candies in his coat pocket and liked to slip me a few dollars on the side; even he betrayed me. They passed you around like a basketball and Uncle Harold jiggled you on his knees. Then it came my turn to hold you. They made me sit all propped up with a pillow at my back, they were so scared I was gonna drop you.

MICHAEL: You couldn't possibly remember all that! You were only three years old!

KEITH: I'm telling you, I remember. You were the ugliest damn thing! You looked like some kind of genetic mutation, all red and wrinkled.

MICHAEL: Thanks a lot.

KEITH: When I went to kiss you, you threw up on me.

MICHAEL: I'm glad.

KEITH: And from then on, that was it. Whatever you did was a million times more thrilling to Mother than any endeavor of mine. They spoiled you rotten. I was never allowed to do things you did when I was your age. Never. You got away with murder all your life. You still do.

MICHAEL: I'd like to get away with one more.

DELORES *bursts out laughing.*

KEITH: What's your problem?

DELORES: You remind me of two baby bear cubs play fighting in the woods: kicking and biting and scratching like mad. I don't suppose it ever crossed your minds that if Mike's Mommy's favorite, and Keith is Dad's, that makes me nobody's favorite.

MICHAEL: Come off it, sis. You're the girl—that makes you immune to most of the crap Keith and I contend with.

DELORES: I can't believe you even had the nerve to say that!

KEITH: Yeah, you always got special treatment.

DELORES: I'll say special treatment. Try having to be in an hour before my older *and* my younger brother just because I'm a girl.

KEITH: So what? Dad's just scared you're gonna make him a grandpa.

DELORES: Well, if he'd talk to me about sex, I could put his mind to rest, but he's way too uptight. I feel like Rapunzel in her tower, only instead of being imprisoned by a witch, I'm guarded by an ogre of a dad.

MICHAEL: All I know is you guys got it easy compared to me.

DELORES: Look! They're starting the finale! *(The sound of fireworks exploding is amplified.)* It's so beautiful, isn't it?

KEITH: Yeah. Listen, Mike, I'm sorry.

MICHAEL: Me too.

DELORES: Let's make a Fourth of July resolution. We're not going to be living home forever. Who knows? In a couple of years we might be scattered all over the world, like seeds of the same strong tree. This is the time we have left to be together. Let's not blow it.

KEITH: Agreed. No more self-pity contests.

MICHAEL: You're right. All for one and one for all. Look at that shower of silver sparks! I think that was the last of it.

KEITH *(raising his bottle to toast)*: To freedom.

DELORES *(raising hers to his)*: To freedom.

MICHAEL *(clinking his bottle against theirs)*: Damn straight.

> *The lights fade on* MIKE, KEITH, *and* DELORES, *and the fender prop is raised once again.* MIKE *exits stage left.* DELORES *and* KEITH *return to the places they had just before the flashback.*

BRIAN: What time is it, anyway? Maybe we should buzz by the hospital and find out what the deal is. They probably wouldn't tell us a thing over the phone.

DELORES: They won't, I'm telling you. But I'd rather wait here, wouldn't you? Someplace familiar. Someplace where Michael spent so many wonderful hours with us.

KEITH: It's nine fifteen. They brought him into the hospital about five hours ago. We'll give it a few hours more. Till twelve o'clock—high noon. Then we'll go. By then it's a safe bet he'll be out of surgery. We'll know one way or another. And if . . . if he never makes it through surgery, I'd rather not know till then.

BONNIE: What'll I do if Michael dies? I love him so much. I can't live without him to love; without him to love me. I'd rather be with him in the grave.

SERENA (*hugging* BONNIE *and gently stroking her hair*): Ssh . . . ssh . . . It's all right, Bonnie. We'll take care of each other. I'm your friend and I care. I'll be your rock. I won't let you drown. I'm here for you. Let me be strong for you and then take the strength from me.

BONNIE: I'm frightened to the marrow of my bones, Serena.

SERENA: I know. It's okay.

BONNIE: You're my best friend. I haven't been very good to you lately, have I? Breaking plans the other night to see Mike, missing your recital last month. I'm really sorry, Ser. I know we haven't spent much time together lately, and that's my fault. Ever since Mike and I hooked up, I guess I just haven't been thinking of much else but him. I took our friendship for granted, and I apologize.

SERENA: I understand.

> SERENA *moves away from* BONNIE *and the others, who freeze. Lights fade on them and come up on the forestage. We hear the offstage*

sound of people at a party: talking, laughing.
SERENA *sits cross-legged on the floor of the*
forestage. Once again rock music announces
MIKE'*s arrival. This time it's Kiss's "See You*
in Your Dreams."

MICHAEL: Hey, sweetheart, what's up? We were
wondering where you disappeared to. This is a
party, remember? You're supposed to be having
fun. You know, party: music, munchies, dancing,
videos. Why are you sitting up here in Bonnie's
bedroom all by yourself?

SERENA *(nastily)*: Why, do you two want the bedroom to yourselves?

MICHAEL: What's that supposed to mean?

SERENA: I don't know why I said that. It was stupid.
I'm sorry.

MICHAEL: Seri, what's going on with you lately?

SERENA: What do you mean?

MICHAEL: You've been acting really weird. Is something bothering you? You seem pissed at me, and
I don't know what I did.

SERENA: It's not you, Mike. It's me. I just have a
lot of things to deal with lately.

MICHAEL: So let's talk.

SERENA: I don't think so.

MICHAEL: Why not? We're friends, aren't we?

SERENA: Yes.

MICHAEL: So? You can trust me.

SERENA: Not with this. It's . . . personal.

MICHAEL: It's about a guy, right?

SERENA: Partly.

MICHAEL: Who?

SERENA: I'd rather not say.

MICHAEL: Then I know him.

SERENA: I'd rather not talk about it.

MICHAEL: I'm worried about you, and so is Bonnie.

SERENA (*sarcastically*): Oh sure. Bonnie's real concerned about me.

MICHAEL: She is! She thinks you're mad at her about something.

SERENA: I'm not mad at anybody but myself.

MICHAEL: Then why are the two of us getting vibes like we hurt you somehow? *(SERENA, still sitting cross-legged on the floor, shakes her head and looks down at her fingernails. MICHAEL paces behind her, with his arms crossed in front of his chest. He stops suddenly, taps his fingertip to his lips, points at SERENA's back.)* Oh, I get why you're mad at us!

SERENA *(nervously)*: You do?

MICHAEL: Sure. You said it's got something to do with a guy, right? Hey, I know me and Bonnie have been spending a lot of time together, and I know what great friends you two are. If you're dating somebody and want to talk girl talk with Bonnie, I'll just fade into the background anytime you say.

SERENA *(with a touch of irony)*: Thanks, Mike.

MICHAEL: C'mon. *(Offering her his hand, MIKE helps SERENA up.)* Let's go find Bonnie. I have to tell you, I sure am glad you introduced the two of us. She's really something special. *(MICHAEL puts his arms around SERENA, holds her for a moment, and kisses her cheek.)* And so are you. *(As he moves away from her, offering his hand to her to hold, SERENA remains stock-still.)* What's wrong?

SERENA: Why did you do that?

MICHAEL: Do what?

SERENA: Why did you kiss me just now?

MICHAEL: You're someone I care about. Why shouldn't I be affectionate? You were feeling down—

SERENA: So you figured you'd take pity on me.

MICHAEL: What? No!

SERENA: I don't want you to kiss me again. Ever.

MICHAEL: Okay, okay. I'm sorry. I didn't mean anything by it.

SERENA: I know you didn't. That's why I don't want you to kiss me again.

MICHAEL: Huh?

SERENA: Didn't you ever think that people shouldn't do and say things they don't mean?"

MICHAEL: What is this all about?

SERENA (Sighs.): It's just that . . . well . . . did you ever find yourself in a situation where you felt totally helpless and frustrated? Helpless because you have no control over another person's feelings for you? Frustrated because, as much as you desire to, you can't modify your own? Well, that's how I feel. I'm angry and jealous and I hate myself for feeling this way!

MICHAEL: Angry and jealous of whom?

SERENA *(exasperated)*: Of you and Bonnie!

MICHAEL: Why?

SERENA: Because, Michael, because she took you away from me and then you took her away from me.

MICHAEL: Oh, Serena!

SERENA: I'm not foolish enough to believe you ever loved me. And I can't pretend I'm surprised you fell for Bonnie. She's beautiful; not just pretty or sexy or cute. Bonnie is beautiful. But do me one favor—don't kiss me or hug me, because now your "affection" hurts. Maybe I was just naive. *(Laughs at herself.)* Obviously so. You see, I really liked you. And you made me think you liked me too: kissing my cheek whenever we'd say good-bye and putting your arm around my shoulder as we walked down the street. I like to think you might have grown to truly care for me, if I hadn't been so shortsighted as to introduce you to my best friend.

Guess I deserve what I got for believing fairy tales still come true. Maybe introducing you to Bonnie was my subconscious scheme to test your loyalty, or hers. In my heart I must have known what would happen. Guys always look at Bonnie first. They never forget her name. I'm always "That girl Bonnie hangs out with." I'm a mushroom growing in the shadow of a rose.

MICHAEL: Serena, I'm sorry. I had no idea.

SERENA: Course not.

MICHAEL: But you shouldn't talk about yourself like that. It isn't true. You're smart and sweet and lovely.

SERENA: Notice the order of the three. My intellect thanks you; my vanity's not so sure.

MICHAEL: You're very hard on yourself for no good reason. Look, I'm sorry if I gave you the wrong impression. You're a warm, friendly person, and it was easy to feel close to you. I didn't mean for you to get the wrong idea.

SERENA: I know. I wish I hadn't told you this. And I wish I didn't feel this clawing at my heart every time I look in your eyes. I've lost out twice. Not only have I lost you, I've lost Bonnie. We promised each other once that no guy would ever come between us. That's why I never admitted to her how I felt about you once I saw she'd fallen. But in losing you, I lost her too. She abandoned me to be your girl. I don't know which hurts more.

MICHAEL: Please say you know I never meant to cause you pain. Tell me you're my friend and that you'll straighten things out with Bonnie.

SERENA: Don't tell her. Please, Michael. Promise.

MICHAEL: Not if you don't want me to.

SERENA: I don't. Don't tell her I cared for you too deeply. Don't let her know I miss spending time with her like we used to before you became the center of her universe. Above all, don't tell her how lonely and selfish I've become.

MICHAEL: I do think you're very beautiful—inside and out.

SERENA: Promise you'll try to forget this confession. Promise me, Michael.

MICHAEL: If that's what you want.

SERENA: What I want wasn't meant to be. Silence is the best alternative. Let's find Bonnie.

> *The lights go out on the couple.* MICHAEL *exits quickly, and* SERENA *returns to her place on the bus seat. Lights come up on the cast again, and they unfreeze.*

BONNIE: What do people leave behind when they die? A few disjointed memories burned into the souls of those who loved them. A photographic image here and there. Garments perfumed with a unique human scent that exists no more in this world. A thought. A poem. A painting. A song. Mourners rushed by time's sands to forget their grief, or at least bury it, pay their faint homage and then let it pass.

Sometimes I think I can feel the spirits of the dead brush past me, like wind rustles through leafy treetops. Certain houses just have that feel, and calm bodies of water always seem to me so mysterious and powerful.

When my grandfather died, I was six. Death, I reasoned, was cause for celebration. When God got lonely for one of his children, he sent a bright angel to fetch his beloved. There was never any doubt in my mind that I'd see my grandfather again. My parents had told me so, and so I couldn't comprehend their tears.

The night after the burial I lay in my bed with my eyes closed after having said my prayers. I thought about my grandpa so intensely that I thought I heard his voice inside my head. Footsteps crossed the bedroom floor and I felt a sudden heaviness upon the bed as if someone had sat down on its edge. I sensed that if I opened my eyes, this visitor would vanish.

When I told my parents about the strange visitation, they looked at each other with panicked concern. I was sent to a psychiatrist till I denounced my grandpa's ghost and declared his presence had been a figment of my imagination. It was then God died in my mind, for if my grandpa's spirit coming to look in on me was such an absurdity, then the miracles of God's love were nothing more than empty, idiotic tales. Yet . . . I like to believe in ghosts and I'm sad that God has died.

SERENA: God hasn't died. God isn't an animal or a human. God is a concept. God is order and reason and light. Order and reason and light are eternal.

BONNIE: In an age of nuclear weaponry, chemical warfare, environmental decay, global overpopulation, random violence, and rampant deadly disease, I'd hardly say God has much of a foothold.

SERENA: You should have more faith.

BONNIE: In God?

SERENA: In mankind's capacity to find the God in all of us. To salvage that sputtering flame of truth and serenity and knowledge that the world strives to extinguish daily. To stay human in the best and brightest sense of the word, no matter how difficult it seems.

BONNIE: I did have faith in one thing: my love for Michael Redhawk. Now he may leave me forever. Faith! Faith is only a wistful desire to believe in miracles, and miracles are rarer than unicorns in Central Park.

KEITH: But not unheard of. I'm gonna believe in miracles. I'm gonna keep believing that we're going to walk through the glass doors of that hospital and my brother will have made it out of surgery just fine; no brain damage, legs bruised a bit but not shattered beyond repair. It isn't such a crazy thing to hope for. People have walked away from plane crashes, right? So walking away from a motorcycle accident isn't such a big deal.

BRIAN: I can't stop thinking this whole thing is mostly my fault. I'm the one who sold Mikey the bike. I'm the one who taught him to ride. If it weren't for me, he might never have gotten hurt. His mother always said I was a bad influence on him. Maybe she was right. We really liked doing dangerous things together. We played reckless games like dashing across the railroad tracks when we saw the lights of a train. There was this pit where the neighborhood kids rode their bicycles. We'd plunge down one side, pick up speed, and come flying out of the hole into a jump or a three sixty. We used to take turns lying down on the ground and letting each other jump over our bodies with the bike.

The other characters freeze and the lights change the mood. The spotlight is on BRIAN *as he moves toward the forestage. Smoke curls about his legs.*

BRIAN: It was all just fun and adventure. Part of being young. There's a terrific thrill in facing what you fear. I know that Bonnie chick is way off base thinking that Mike was trying to off himself. Mike loved danger, but he loved life more.

As BRIAN *continues his monologue, stagehands assemble the overpass prop. The prop might consist of a wall of sturdy wooden boxes painted to resemble the stones of a highway overpass. The wall should stretch at least nine feet across the stage if not more, and rise about four or five feet in height. The actors should be able to maneuver across its top, but not easily. A width of about two feet should be ample. A chain link fence rises up from behind the wall and stretches its length.*

BRIAN: Everyone wonders what it'll be like to die, and a lot of people think about killing themselves, too. I'll bet a lot more than you'd think. A lot more than who will admit it. Only idiots are happy all the time. But you turn up your collar and you blink back the tears and you fight. And Mikey's a fighter like me. I have proof he didn't want to die.

The stage fades to black for a few moments. This time the music introducing the flashback is AC-DC's "Highway to Hell." After a while the sounds of a busy highway crescendo and level off. We hear: car horns, the rattle of large trucks going by, the whoosh of winds created by the larger vehicles, the deep bellow of truck horns and the friction of tires on blacktop. The lights come up on BRIAN *and* MICHAEL, *who are atop the wall.* MICHAEL *is at the end of the wall stage left, with his back to the audience, clinging to the fence.* BRIAN *stands to his left facing the audience with a look of absolute terror plastered on his face, fingers laced through the holes in the fence. A particularly loud rattle, as of an eighteen-wheeler passing by, makes them cringe simultaneously.*

BRIAN: Hey dude! Hey dude! You okay?

MICHAEL *(squeaking)*: Sure, just fine!

BRIAN: You know what, buddy? I'm beginning to have serious second thoughts about this brainstorm of mine.

MICHAEL: You don't say?

BRIAN: Maybe we should just climb back over this fence and forget the whole thing.

155

MICHAEL: I'm with you.

BRIAN: Okay. You want to go first or should I?

MICHAEL: I'll go first. (MICHAEL *turns around to face the audience. He glances down. Suddenly his eyes go wide and he grimaces. He speaks through clenched teeth.*) Bri? Dude? I think maybe you should go first.

BRIAN: I can't move.

MICHAEL: If we climbed over one side, we can climb back over the other. It's just the same. Now you just climb back over the fence nice and easy and slow and then walk down the ramp to the phone.

BRIAN: The phone?

MICHAEL: Tell the fire department to set up a block-ade and get the hook and ladder down here like yesterday.

BRIAN (*looking down, then cringing*): It sure didn't seem so high up looking up as it does looking down.

MICHAEL: I can't believe I let you talk me into this. If we get out of this alive, it'll be the last thing you ever do.

BRIAN: What are you talking about? This was as much your idea as it was mine.

MICHAEL: What?!

BRIAN: You're the one who said that advertising is vital to the success of a band.

MICHAEL: I was talking about flyers, mailing lists, publicity shots. I never said a word about imitating Spiderman.

BRIAN: But just think, if we spray paint the band's logo on the overpass, millions of people will see it.

MICHAEL: Lot of good that does a dead man.

BRIAN: So long as we're up here, we might as well try.

MICHAEL: Okay, okay. One of us will paint it and the other will hold on to him to make sure he keeps his balance. Deal?

BRIAN: Deal. Loser does the logo. Odds or evens?

MICHAEL: Odds.

BRIAN: Once—twice—three . . . shoot! (BRIAN *and* MICHAEL *open their clenched fists simultaneously in the imitation of shooting dice.* BRIAN *is showing one finger;* MICHAEL, *two.*) Odds, you win. Now, hold tight, man. Okay?

> BRIAN *and* MICHAEL *shuffle across the wall till they come center.* BRIAN *lies down on the ledge.* MICHAEL *holds the fence with one hand and* BRIAN's *wrist with the other.* BRIAN *leans down over the edge and starts to paint "Redhawk."*

MICHAEL: Now remember, make sure you paint it upside down and backward.

BRIAN: Right.

MICHAEL: And don't look down.

BRIAN: How am I supposed to write it if I don't look down?

MICHAEL: Look down, but just don't look too far down.

BRIAN: You just make sure you've got a tight grip on me.

MICHAEL: I won't let you fall. *(BRIAN finishes the logo, but it reads "Rebhawk," not "Redhawk," because he was so nervous. The stage fades to black once again, and when the lights come up, MICHAEL and BRIAN are standing on the forestage, looking at the wall.)* I don't believe it. I just don't believe it after all that. Rebhawk! Rebhawk!

BRIAN: Come on, what do you want from me? So I made a little mistake. It's not easy writing upside down and backward with these gigantic trucks whizzing past your skull.

MICHAEL: Redhawk. R-e-d-h-a-w-k. How difficult can it be?

BRIAN: Then you should have done the logo.

MICHAEL: Obviously.

BRIAN: We could always change the name of the band.

MICHAEL: Are you serious? My name's Redhawk, not Rebhawk.

BRIAN: Rebhawk's not so bad.

MICHAEL: It sounds like an Alabama-based airline.

BRIAN: So fix the logo! Go climb up there and fix it if you're so smart.

MICHAEL: Why don't you?

BRIAN: Why don't you?

MICHAEL: Chicken?

BRIAN: No. You?

MICHAEL: No. *(Pause.)* Actually, Rebhawk isn't so bad. Sort of has that rock-'n'-roll rebel connotation.

BRIAN: Yeah. I was thinking that too.

MICHAEL: We could shoot odds or evens to see who goes up there to fix it.

BRIAN: We could.

MICHAEL: Or we could just think about using the name Rebhawk.

BRIAN: Sure. Or we could always come back here tomorrow.

MICHAEL: Yeah, that's an idea.

BRIAN: Yeah.

MICHAEL: Bri?

BRIAN: Yup.

MICHAEL: Let's never do this again.

BRIAN: Not in a million years. *(The stage fades to black. The wall is disassembled.* MICHAEL *leaves the stage and* BRIAN *resumes his place.)* I never should have taught him how to ride.

DELORES: Courage. Did you know that's what my mother wanted to name Michael when he was born? Courage Redhawk. Of course my father wouldn't think of it. "Too theatrical," he said. Michael was born early, and he was in an incubator for the first two weeks of his life. He struggled to stay alive. My mother said that was bravery. My father called it instinct. Now he clings to life and I wonder too if it's courage or instinct.

SERENA: Maybe bravery is just instinct carried to the extreme.

BONNIE: It takes a great deal of courage to ride straight into death's dark mouth.

KEITH: That's it! I've had it with you, Bonnie. Just what are you trying to do? You keep talking about my brother like he's some kind of suicidal maniac, and he isn't! Mike's got problems like everyone else, but nothing worth killing himself over. Including you! *(Scoffingly)* Miss Wax-Perfect Juliet Capulet. You think no one notices the way you try to control my brother? I never liked you. You're bad for Michael. I tried to tell him that, but he wouldn't listen. Just what are you after, anyway?

BONNIE: I'm not after anything . . . except maybe the truth.

KEITH *(sarcastically)*: Oh, the truth. I see now. You're going to tell us the truth about Michael. You, some little off-the-corner moon-eyed bimbo, are going to tell me the deep dark truth about my only brother.

BRIAN: Lay off it, man. That's out of hand.

KEITH: No! No, that's not out of hand. I'm sick and tired of this crazy chick trying to convince us that Mike tried to do himself in, and I won't have her running around school spreading that kind of ugly rumor about my bro.

BONNIE: What are you really afraid of, Keith? Are you afraid that if it turns out my love tried to kill himself, you might have to shoulder part of the blame?

KEITH: You're a mental case.

BONNIE: What if we're all to blame? You and Delores and Serena. Brian and I. Even Painter, the artist, for not creating something perfect enough to flood Mike's senses with beauty and grace. To give him courage and fortitude enough to keep swimming against the tide.

KEITH: You always talk in riddles. That's another thing I never liked about you.

BONNIE: Then I'll speak plainly. I think Michael was tired of living. I believe he's a manic-depressive. One minute he's up; the next, he's down. Like me. Except it kept getting harder and harder to pull himself up by his bootstraps. It got harder and harder to keep the faith. He just got worn with living, like a piece of glass tossed by waves eventually gets smooth and milky and loses its jagged edge. Mike lost his edge. He just couldn't face another empty dawn, so he rode right into it, riding out the storm.

KEITH: You're a liar!

BONNIE: I love him! I can't help but love him, and you know I'm only saying what you've thought. We . . . all of us . . . let him down. We weren't compassionate enough. We didn't listen carefully enough to what he was trying to say. Something happened we . . . I . . . should have foreseen. In his mind, a moment in time appeared where he could escape, so he took the out.

KEITH: No!

BONNIE: Haven't you thought about it yourself?

KEITH: Why don't you get the hell out of here?!

DELORES: Keith, stop it! And that's enough out of you too, Bonnie. None of this matters! What was going on in his mind that split second before the . . . crash . . . it doesn't matter. What matters is that he's still alive.

BONNIE: But it does matter. Don't you see? It matters because if his spirit is wounded along with his body, physical therapy might heal the one, but the other aches most deeply. It's deadly.

BRIAN: You know what I think? I think Mike was just out having a good time. He loved to ride. It rejuvenated him. It kept him from going nuts. Maybe he had a lot on his mind. Maybe the only way he could relax was to take the bike out. Some jerk probably didn't see him in the rain, cut him off, and sent him into the guardrail.

SERENA: That makes sense, Bonnie. Listen to Brian. It doesn't do anyone any good to feel responsible. None of us is to blame.

KEITH: Maybe one of us *is* to blame. Maybe one of

us delights in pointing the finger at all of us
because she doesn't want to bear the burden of
her guilt alone.

SERENA: Don't, Keith. . . .

KEITH *(Walks up to* BONNIE *and talks to her closely and
almost seductively. It is obvious he is invading her personal
space.)*:   One of us tried to break Michael in like
a wild mustang. You know how you break in an
untamed animal? You break its spirit. Break his
spirit and you break the rest of him.

BONNIE: It was never like that.

KEITH: Wasn't it?

BONNIE: No!

KEITH: You tried to lure my brother into your web
with your fawning words and your perfumed hair.
You had nothing to offer him. All you did was
make things more complicated for him.

BONNIE *(visibly shaken)*:   I loved Michael. I love Michael.

KEITH: You see? In your mind he's already dead,
because you stole away his spontaneity, his freedom. Isn't that true?!

BONNIE: You don't know me. You don't know anything about me. And you sure don't know the first thing about my relationship with your brother.

KEITH: I know you changed him.

BONNIE: Not by much and only for the better.

KEITH: Then why is he lying in a hospital bed?

SERENA: Cut it out, Keith. Please! Can't you see she's had enough? When you hurt her like this, you wound me too, and I never did anything to you.

KEITH *(ignoring* SERENA*)*: You filled my brother's head with all kinds of psychological garbage, Bonnie. You burrowed under his skin and stayed there, like a blood-gorged tick.

BONNIE: I don't have to take this from you! Come on, Serena. Let's go. We'll wait for word at the hospital.

KEITH: Good riddance! *(*KEITH *picks up* BONNIE*'s looseleaf and the book that lies beside it on the ground by the bus seat.)* And take this with you. *(*KEITH *glances at the title.) The Poems of John Clare.* More meaningless intellectual babble, no doubt.

BONNIE: Give me that!

> SERENA *grabs the book away, and an envelope falls to the ground. She picks up the envelope and her hand steals to her mouth.*

KEITH: What?! What is it?

BONNIE: It's a sealed envelope. My name's written on it . . . in Michael's hand.

DELORES: Read it to us, Bonnie.

BONNIE: I'm afraid.

> *The other characters freeze. The lighting changes to that muted, otherworld effect. A fog machine would enhance the scene with swirls of mist enveloping prop tombstones to give the impression of a moonlit graveyard.*

BONNIE: I'm afraid to know.

> BONNIE *stares straight ahead as if in a trance. The letter slips from her fingers.* MIKE *enters stage right, retrieves the envelope, and slips it into the back pocket of his jeans. He puts the*

book into the inside pocket of his leather jacket. Aerosmith's ballad "Angel" is played in part, during which time MIKE *sits on a tombstone and drinks a bottle of red wine.* BONNIE *comes out of her reverie and approaches* MIKE *with excitement and happiness.*

BONNIE: I was afraid you wouldn't wait for me.

MICHAEL: Baby! *(*MIKE *embraces* BONNIE.*)* What happened? I've been waiting so long.

BONNIE: I'm sorry. It's my father again. He got home before I could get to the mail, and he found a letter from you to me.

MICHAEL: Crap!

BONNIE: Can you believe he actually had the nerve to open it up and read it! I hate that he invaded my privacy like that. He's got no right!

MICHAEL: What I wrote was meant for your eyes only.

BONNIE: He already told me he doesn't want me seeing you anymore. I don't care what he wants. He never listens to anything I say. He doesn't understand me, he doesn't care. And then he has the nerve to order me around and tell me how to live. He thinks he owns me.

MICHAEL: Take it easy, love. You're with me now.

BONNIE *(pacing)*: He makes me so angry I could spit! He just wants to ruin my life. He said if he caught me going out with you, he'd throw me out of the house. I don't care if he does. He threw my sister out, too. I'll go live with her. Or maybe with my grandparents. I could get my own place if I had to!

MICHAEL: Forget about him. You know he's not going to throw you out.

BONNIE: I lied to him. I told him I was going over to Serena's to study. He knew I was lying, but I don't care.

MICHAEL: It's no use trying to please them . . . parents, I mean . . . trying to make them respect you. They never do. They just force you out into the world whether you want to be there or not, and then they harass you and belittle you and pound on your eggshell ego. They're so much bigger than you for so many, many years. They threaten and twist you and try to make you their demented puppet. Once in a while they tell you they love you, just to confuse the situation. It's worse when you love them back.

BONNIE: You've been drinking.

MICHAEL *(taking a swig of wine)*: Drinking . . . thinking . . . linking . . . sinking.

BONNIE: You shouldn't drink when you're down.

MICHAEL: You shouldn't nag when I'm down. *(Seeing the hurt look on her face)* I'm sorry, I didn't mean that. I'm just so tired of all the garbage I go through every day.

BONNIE: Like?

MICHAEL: Like school, for one thing. People always telling me what to do . . . "preparing me for the future" . . . what a joke. It's more like brainwashing me into believing I'm just another cog in the corporate machine. Trying to take away my power, my individuality. Telling me what to read . . . what to say . . . what to believe.

BONNIE: You should try not to let it bother you. You won't be in school forever.

MICHAEL: Don't you get it? There'll always be some

creep trying to tell me what to do; whether it's my parents, or my teachers, or a boss, or a record producer.

BONNIE: That's the answer there. You should spend more time on your music.

MICHAEL: It's not *my* music. That's the point! That's another reason I'm so miserable. I can't write! I'm just the singer, just a hired gun. Jimmy and Spider write the songs.

BONNIE: You've got to learn to relax, Mike. You're driving yourself nuts over things you can't control! If you weren't so uptight and self-conscious, maybe you'd be able to write. You worry too much.

MICHAEL: I can't help it! I try, but it's useless. My own anger and fear and hate hang over my head like a great, gloomy cloud. I dwell on the past all the time. I can't forgive myself for the things I did when I was younger. And I get so frustrated living day to day, feeling like I'm just running on a treadmill that's gradually speeding up. No matter how exhausted I get, I have to run faster and faster just to keep up. Just to save myself from falling. Whenever I think about the future, I get knots in my stomach. I think about the big issues, like will I get sent off to some little-known country to fight some bigwig's war? Will the earth survive man's ecological devastation? How many people will die of AIDS in the years to come? And then I worry about things that are admittedly unimportant. I ask myself, "What if this happens . . . what if that happens?" creating more bogeymen out of boredom or nervousness.

BONNIE: Oh, Michael!

MICHAEL: I truly wish I'd never been born. I didn't ask for this. I'm scared to die, but I'm afraid of how I'll change if I live. I don't want to bite and claw my way through life. So many people live that way, like too many rats in too small a cage.

BONNIE (embracing MICHAEL): You're only seeing one side of life, darling. There is so much beauty that surrounds us. Look at that silvery moon up there! Sickle sharp! Encased by swirling clouds tinged a glowing bronze. Isn't it beautiful? Close your eyes and feel the gentle breeze tiptoe across your skin. Doesn't it feel wonderful? I love the way I see the world when I'm with you.

MICHAEL: I wish I could see the world the way you

do. Sometimes you give me a little glimpse of it when you talk this way. Sometimes I see a spark of it in your eyes. When I was a child, I saw the world that way.

BONNIE: When you were a child, you weren't afraid to play. That's what's wrong now. You carry the world's woes upon your shoulder like you were dragging a cross. You've got to give it up. Michael, face the fact that your outrage and sense of justice alone can't save the world. Every day, you live your life the best way you know how. You learn something new. You do some small thing to make someone else's life a little better. You do something that feels meaningful to your own life. You play. You laugh. You grow. You can't expect much more from yourself, now can you?

MICHAEL: I'd say I wish you understood, but I'm glad you don't share my despair.

BONNIE: Michael, I do understand. Don't you think I get scared and angry and hurt? I've felt everything you're feeling and just as deeply. But you can't let it beat you!

MICHAEL: If only I weren't so alone.

BONNIE: You're really not.

MICHAEL: Look out across the field there, Bonnie, and tell me what you see. Let me see the world again through your innocent eyes. *(BONNIE moves to the very front of the forestage, looking out across the audience.)*

BONNIE: Tombstones. Rows and rows of markers. Tiny lights shining through the mist. Those little candles that stand like miniature shrines, they must be. *(Spotlight on MICHAEL as he takes the letter from his pocket and looks at it in turmoil.)* The mist is rising up into such strange shapes. I don't think I like the looks of that one. It looks like . . . Oh no, but that's ridiculous. *(MICHAEL takes the book of Clare's poetry out, kisses the letter, and slips it between the pages of the book.)* It's getting cold, Michael, isn't it? *(Shivers.)* I feel suddenly very cold. And the wind is rising. A damp, chill wind. *(MICHAEL presses the book to his chest, and a great crash of thunder resounds. BONNIE turns to him.)* There's a storm coming. We have to get home.

MICHAEL: Yes. I must get home. Here, take this. Thanks for lending it to me.

BONNIE: You liked it?

MICHAEL: Yes.

BONNIE: I hadn't finished it myself. I'll bring it to school tomorrow and finish it in study hall.

MICHAEL: I'll give you a ride to your house.

BONNIE: No, I'd better run home. I don't want my father to hear the motorcycle pull up. It will only make things worse, and my house is just a block away.

MICHAEL: Here. Take this. *(MICHAEL takes the talisman that hangs about his neck and puts it around BONNIE's.)*

BONNIE: But this is your good-luck charm! You never take it off.

MICHAEL: I want you to keep it.

BONNIE: I don't understand.

MICHAEL: I have to leave you now.

BONNIE: You act as though you were going some-place you weren't coming back from. *(Thunder booms and the lights flash, imitating lightning.)*

MICHAEL: I'll never stop loving you.

BONNIE: Michael?!

MICHAEL: Good-bye!

Either MICHAEL *gets on his bike onstage and rides off, or he walks offstage and the sound of a motorcycle engine is heard—whichever the stage and cast can accommodate.* BONNIE *returns to the place where she was standing before the flashback. She holds the book and drops the letter on the floor as she had before.*

BONNIE: Afraid.

BRIAN: Then I'll read it. *(Scoops up the letter.)*

BONNIE: No! Give it back! *(*BONNIE *grabs away the envelope. She looks at it for a few moments and then opens it and reads a few lines and half sobs, half sighs.)* Oh, Michael.

DELORES: Bonnie, read it!

BONNIE *(reading)*: "Dear Bonnie, Delores, Keith, Brian, Serena, Painter, Mom, and Dad:

"If you are reading this, it means that I finally got up the nerve to do something I've been thinking about for a long, long time. I hope I went quickly and cleanly and that none of you had to see anything too gruesome.

"I love you all very much. Nothing is anyone's fault. I'm very tired, that's all. So tired I could sleep forever. Please take care of my parrot, Pop-eye. He always liked you best, Brian; so maybe you should take him. Popeye loves sunflower seeds, don't forget.

"Please try to remember me those times I was at my best. Not all of the journey was dark. Remember me through the things I loved best: sunsets and strawberries, music and movies, riding and romancing. Keep the faith I lost and forgive me.

"Michael Redhawk"

The book's dog-eared at the place where Michael hid the letter. This poem's starred:

"I AM
"by John Clare

"I am: yet what I am none cares or knows,
    My friends forsake me like a memory lost;
I am the self-consumer of my woes,
    They rise and vanish in oblivious host,
Like shades in love and death's oblivion lost;
And yet I am, and live with shadows tost.

"Into the nothingness of scorn and noise,
    Into the living sea of waking dreams,

Where there is neither sense of life nor joys,
But the vast shipwreck of my life's esteems;
And e'en the dearest—that I loved the best—
Are strange—nay, rather stranger than the rest.

"I long for scenes where man has never trod;
A place where woman never smiled or wept;
There to abide with my Creator, God,
And sleep as I in childhood sweetly slept:
Untroubling and untroubled where I lie;
The grass below—above the vaulted sky."

KEITH *(after a long silence)*: It's only words on paper. He isn't gone yet.

BRIAN: That's right. I'll bet the second before it happened, Mike changed his mind: tried to avoid the crash. That's why he's still alive. Because he chose to be.

SERENA: Painter's finished his painting.

PAINTER: Do you know what it's an image of?

DELORES *(inspecting the work closer)*: Yes. I know what it is. It's the phoenix bird, rising from the ashes of its own decay. It dies in flames and it is reborn from the same embers.

BRIAN *(to* PAINTER*)*: You meant this as more than color splashed on a crumbling wall.

PAINTER: Yes. It's for Michael.

BONNIE: But what does it symbolize? A perished soul reborn into a new existence? Or a wounded spirit healed through its own inner strength?

PAINTER: I am only the artist. That is for you to decide. *(The characters remain on stage for a moment, contemplating the mural. The sound of bells echoes across the stage.)*

SERENA: High noon.

KEITH *(to* BONNIE, *of all people)*: Ready?

BONNIE: Yeah.

> BRIAN *and* DELORES *exit stage right.* SERENA *and* PAINTER *exit stage right. Lights fade to a muted solemn color, spotlight on the phoenix mural and on the wildflowers blooming from the base of the crumbling wall.* BONNIE *reaches down to pick them, sharing the stage with* KEITH *only.*

KEITH: Don't.

BONNIE: I was going to bring them to the hospital, to Michael.

KEITH: Yeah?

BONNIE: I want him to see something beautiful when he wakes up . . . something graceful and pure and genuine.

KEITH: It's so hard for anything beautiful to survive this world. Let it live.

> BONNIE *stands up straight and looks* KEITH *in the eyes. They share a smile, glance at the mural as they leave, and exit stage right. The spotlight remains on the wildflowers as Andy Taylor's "Don't Let Me Die Young" plays itself out, and the stage fades to black.*

CURTAIN

CIN FORSHAY-LUNSFORD

When she was a seventeen-year-old senior at Lynbrook High School on Long Island, New York, Cin Forshay-Lunsford began writing what eventually was published as *Walk Through Cold Fire*. In her novel a sixteen-year-old middle-class girl, much like Cin herself, leaves home searching for her place in the world and finds it with a teenage gang. Its publication resulted in her being named one of the top one hundred teens in America by *Teen-Age* magazine.

As a child Forshay-Lunsford was taken to plays, ballets, and operas by her mother (who is an English professor). In high school she joined the drama club but ended up painting scenery and being given bit parts in *Oklahoma*, *The Sound of Music*, and *The Crucible*, eventually playing Eve in a student production of *The Diary of Adam and Eve*. As a senior she wrote and directed her own original work, *Guitar Songs*, which was performed at Lynbrook High School in 1983.

Believing that "so many creative things can come from turning one's back on convention and tending to the realm of imagination," Cin Forshay-Lunsford has published two short stories for teenagers and has completed a collection of her own poems written between 1979 and 1988. Among the plants, seashells, crystals, candles, and books in her cluttered studio in Oceanside, New York, in the company of several pets, she is currently at work on a fantasy novel called *The Emerald Sea Princess*.

LARGE FEARS, LITTLE DEMONS

by Dallin Malmgren

CHARACTERS

CASSIE TATE, a fifteen-year-old

MR. TATE, Cassie's father

MRS. TATE, Cassie's mother

NEAL, Cassie's ten-year-old brother

REV. BECKLEY, a young minister

SHELLY, Cassie's best friend

TOMMY, a classmate

SETTING

The stage is divided into three areas of a suburban home. On the left is the small kitchen; in the center is the living room; and on the right is CASSIE's bedroom. As the play opens, the kitchen is lit and MR. TATE is making coffee and mixing pancake batter. MRS. TATE is in the bedroom, which is dimly lit, sitting on the side of CASSIE's bed. They are talking inaudibly.

MR. TATE (*stepping into living room and calling out*): Breakfast will be ready in fifteen minutes! Last one down is a rotten egg! Second to last has to eat it!

> CASSIE *stirs on her bed, and* MRS. TATE *stands up. She pats* CASSIE *on the head, but* CASSIE *seems to retreat farther under her covers.* MRS. TATE *leaves.*

CASSIE (*irritably*): Shut the door! Oh, damn.

> CASSIE's *ten-year-old brother comes down the stairway and, dropping to his knees, sneaks into his sister's room and under her bed.* MRS. TATE *has moved across the stage into the kitchen.*

MRS. TATE: Let me guess—buckwheat pancakes.

MR. TATE: Keep you regular as clockwork. Where're the kids?

MRS. TATE: Neal'll be down soon. (*She hesitates.*) Cassie won't be eating.

MR. TATE: What's the matter? She sick? (MRS. TATE *glares at him.*) No, of course not. It's the dream.

MRS. TATE: She had it again, Frank. And today is the fifth of April.

MR. TATE: And yesterday was the fourth and to-morrow will be the sixth. Nothing's going to change that.

MRS. TATE: She just thinks it would be safer to stay in bed today. I'm not sure I disagree with her.

MR. TATE: I know you don't. That's what drives me crazy! She's going to miss school today because she feels safer lying in her canopied bed, and her own mother's going to hold her hand and pat her forehead, saying, "There, there, honey, you're safe from those nasty ol' dreams, which are only in your head anyway." What're you going to do when she dreams that a whole month is danger-ous? Or a year?

MRS. TATE *(resignedly)*: I don't know, Frank. You bet-ter flip your pancakes. I knew you hated that canopy.

> *The lighting dims in the kitchen and brightens in* CASSIE's *room. She stirs, peeks out from under the covers, then sits up against the head-board. She faces a giant stuffed panda bear, sitting in like manner at the other end of the bed.*

CASSIE: I don't care what they say, Pandy, nothing will get me out of this bed today. If fate or God or whatever has decided that my number is up, then they're gonna have to march right in here and get me, because I'm not moving. Dad can give me as many dirty looks as he wants. Life is an accident waiting to happen. Let's suppose that I did make it to school safely, a considerable feat in itself. How do I know there's not some psycho who hasn't chosen today to bring a pistol to class and open fire. Heck, I think Stevie Sjoberg fits that description nicely. Of course, everybody else thinks I'm the one who's crazy. I don't think Dad even believes I really have the dream. He probably thinks I just want to skip school. What do you think, Pandy? Am I crazy?

NEAL *(from under the bed)*: No, I think it's perfectly normal to ask a teddy bear for advice!

CASSIE *(Looks shocked for an instant, then shrieks.)*: Neal!! You brat! You could have given me a heart attack. Get out of here!

NEAL *(crawling out from under the bed)*: So you really think you're safe in your bedroom, huh, Cass? Must not have seen *Poltergeist. (He plays an air guitar and leaves the room singing.)* "Nowhere to run to, baby, nowhere to hide."

CASSIE: Even my family's a danger. When God ran out of insects, He invented little brothers. *(She slides under her covers.* MR. TATE *comes into the room, looks around.)*

MR. TATE: Excuse me, Pandemonium, have you seen the little girl who lives in this room? My company is having a sale this month on fallout shelters, and I thought she might be interested. *(There is no movement on the bed.)* You can't imagine how safe it is in a fallout shelter. I tell you those things are as cozy as a coffin.

CASSIE *(from under the covers)*: You're not funny, Dad.

MR. TATE: Who's being funny? You're the one who would rather hide from your problems than face them. Sounds like a fallout shelter kind of life to me.

CASSIE: It's easy for you to be brave—it's not your dream. I wonder how you'd feel if I did get up and act like it was a normal day, and then got killed on the way to school.

MR. TATE: You know how I'd feel. But do you really think that's going to happen?

CASSIE: I don't know what's gonna happen! That's why I'm not getting out of bed. You know what happened with Grandma after I dreamed about her.

MR. TATE: Cassie, that was a long time ago, and your grandmother was dying anyway. You didn't dream her into the grave. If anything, your dream was just a response to what was going on around you.

CASSIE: But I didn't know she was dying. Not until I dreamed it.

MR. TATE: Maybe you knew more than you realized.

CASSIE: What about Chaos?

MR. TATE: Contrary to legend, cats only get one life, just like the rest of us. Chaos made the bad decision of trying to cross the street at the same time a car was using it. Simple physics.

CASSIE: What about my dream?

MR. TATE *(gently)*:   You didn't tell us about that

dream until after Chaos was dead. Maybe you mixed up the dates a little.

CASSIE (*angrily*): I knew it! You never believed me. You probably don't believe I'm having this dream either. You think I'm crazy!

MR. TATE: Not at all. I don't question the dream at all, just your response to it. No one can control everything that goes on in her mind. But we can control how we react to it. I think you're behaving irrationally.

CASSIE: See! You think I'm crazy.

MR. TATE: I didn't say that. I just think you're letting your emotions run your life. Don't worry, it runs in our family. But I know, and I think you know, that the sensible thing to do is get up from this bed and get on with your day.

CASSIE: Are you ordering me to go to school?

MR. TATE (*laughing*): Oh no, I'm not making it that easy for you. You're fifteen years old. You're capable of making this decision yourself.

CASSIE (*scrunching down defiantly*): Then I'm not going.

MR. TATE (*disturbed*): Suit yourself. But you're not

lying in bed watching soap operas all day either. *(He walks to the bureau and unplugs her portable TV and lifts it.)* I'm a little disappointed in you, Cassie. *(He leaves.)*

CASSIE *(to Pandy)*: Better a live disappointment than a dead hero. *(She throws back the covers and sits cross-legged facing the panda bear.)* So Dad says I'm ir-rational. According to my psych teacher at school, Freud said that our dreams were simply a form of wish fulfillment. I guess that means I'm really suicidal. Funny, I don't feel suicidal. I feel like I'm clinging to life. But Jung believed our dreams were a way of coping with reality and that they could be connected to our psychic powers. I guess he'd tell me to stay right where I am. Hey, that makes me a Jungian. *(She frowns.)* You're not help-ing much, Pandy, sitting there staring at me like some silent Buddha. I wonder what Buddha would say about this.

The lights dim in CASSIE's *room and brighten in the kitchen.*

MR. TATE *(glumly)*: Well, she's staying home.

NEAL: Hey, did I tell you about my dream? The school bus pulls up to my stop, ya know, and the doors open and this big blob that looks like red Jell-O comes oozin' out, and it covers me up. At first it feels good, ya know, but then I taste it and it tastes like that stuff the dentist makes you rinse out your mouth with, and I get scared, ya know—

MRS. TATE: Go and wash up before the real school bus gets here, or I'll put you on a red Jell-O diet. *(NEAL starts to protest, then gets up and goes. To MR. TATE)* You didn't lose your temper with her, did you?

MR. TATE: Hell no. *(He pours his coffee and takes some hotcakes off the platter.)* I did take the TV from her room, though. I don't want to make her day too easy.

MRS. TATE: You can't really think she's just trying to get out of school, can you?

MR. TATE: No, of course not, but that's the end result, isn't it? I just want to make sure she has some time to consider all the consequences of what she's doing.

MRS. TATE: You make it sound so serious. It's just one day of school.

MR. TATE: No, it's not. That isn't the point at all. By staying home today, she's deciding that it's okay to let her fears be the deciding factors in her life. She's relying more on what she doesn't understand than on what she knows. When you do that, you might as well turn in your ID card and start wearing a sign that says, "Who's in charge?"

MRS. TATE: But what if there is, um, a meaning to her dream? You know she had those two other dreams about death.

MR. TATE *(shaking his head in disgust)*: Don't you understand what you're saying? If there were a "meaning" to her dream, as you say—if today were the day she was destined to die, if some supernatural force were behind this—do you really think staying in bed would stop it? That's a pretty little demon you're wrestling with. Uh-uh. The minute I believe her dream is the minute I condemn her to death, and I'm not going to do that.

MRS. TATE *(somberly)*: So what do you think we should do?

MR. TATE: You do what you think is best. I'm going

to do exactly what I wish she would do. Get up, go to work, and treat it like any other day. *(He leaves.)*

> MRS. TATE *sits there without moving for some time. Then, as the lights dim, she gets up, walks to the kitchen phone, and dials a number. She begins talking inaudibly. All lights remained dimmed for a brief time. Then* CASSIE *is jarred awake by the phone ringing next to her bed.*

CASSIE: Hello? Hi, Shelly. . . . No, I was just lying in bed thinking. . . . Yes, it is definitely better than sitting in Mr. Kearn's class. How did you get out of it? . . . What if he checks up on you? . . . Mr. Kearn just might walk in—he's goofy enough. . . . You're kidding! What did you say? . . . He really asked you that? How did he sound when he said it? . . . You are kidding! He never even acted like he noticed me before. If you're just saying this to get me to come to school . . . No, I'm not coming to school! . . . I don't care who asked about me. . . . No, you're the one who doesn't understand. I'm not coming to school because I want to stay alive, so there will be lots of boys like Tommy Haffner in my future. . . . No, Shelly, you tell me. You're my best friend. Do you think there's even the smallest chance I might have some psychic powers? . . . Okay, that's why I'm staying in bed. *(She hangs up the phone. To Pandy)* It will take more than some boy asking about me to get me out of bed today. Seems like most people don't realize how easy it is to die. I've even heard about people slipping in the shower and drowning on the shower floor!

> MRS. TATE *comes to the door to check on* CASSIE.

MRS. TATE: Hello, honey, how are you getting along? Who was on the phone?

CASSIE: I'm okay, Mom. So far, so good. That was Shel.

MRS. TATE: What did she want?

CASSIE: Just checking up on me. Nothing important. Aren't you going to work today?

MRS. TATE: No, I've got everything up to date, and I can use a day off. Listen, hon, I need to tell you something. I called Reverend Beckley at church, and he's coming over to talk with you.

CASSIE *(throwing herself back on the bed and grabbing her forehead)*: Oh God, Mom, why'd you do that? What am I supposed to say to him? He'll think I'm just some goofy teenager.

MRS. TATE: Reverend Beckley is one of the kindest, wisest men I know, even if he is kind of young for a minister. If you hadn't quit going to youth group last year, you'd know that.

CASSIE: But it's embarrassing, Mom. He probably takes it personally that I don't go to youth group anymore. And what can he tell me about the dream?

MRS. TATE: I don't know, but we'll find out. He should be here soon. I think if this problem is serious enough to stay home from school for, then it's serious enough to talk to a minister about. Now, Cassie, when he gets here, why don't you come out and talk to him in the living room?

CASSIE *(vehemently)*: No way! We learned in health class that the bedroom is the safest room in the house. I meant it when I said I'm not getting out of bed today. If Reverend Beckley or anyone else wants to talk to me, they're going to have to come in here.

The doorbell rings.

MRS. TATE: That must be him. Well, if it has to be in your bedroom, that's where it will be.

> MRS. TATE *goes out. She can be seen answering the door at the back of the living room, and talking animatedly but inaudibly with the* REV-EREND, *who mostly just nods his head. In the meantime,* CASSIE *is sitting up in her bed, staring stonily at her panda bear.*

REV. BECKLEY *(knocking lightly at* CASSIE's *door. He is holding a kitchen chair.):* Cassie? May I come in? I'd like to talk.

CASSIE: It's open.

REV. BECKLEY *(Sets the chair by* CASSIE's *bed, then turns it backward and straddles it.):* Hiya, Cassie. Boy, are you growing up! Listen, your mom thought it would be a good idea if we had a talk. Is that all right with you?

CASSIE *(guardedly):* I guess so.

REV. BECKLEY: She didn't say much—just that you've been having a recurring dream that's causing you some concern.

CASSIE *(Laughs humorlessly.)*: I guess you could say that.

REV. BECKLEY: Would you mind describing the dream for me?

CASSIE: I'm tired of talking about it. *(Pauses.)* Oh, all right. The dream is always the same. I wake up in the middle of the night, only I don't really wake up—I'm just dreaming it. And that window's open, which it never is, and this cool breeze is making the lace curtain billow out into the room. There's this eerie light shining through the window too, like blue moonlight. Anyway, I get out of bed, but I don't want to—it's like this force is making me. On the wall over there a calendar's hanging, a fairly big one, with a square for each date, very plain. The blue light in the room seems like it's directed at the white calendar, and I walk up to it. The calendar says April, and there's a big red circle around Thursday, the fifth. I see some writing within the circle, so I lean closer to see what it says. I see the words, printed very plainly in block letters: "THE DAY YOU DIE!" Then I wake up.

REV. BECKLEY: That does sound frightening. How many times have you had the dream?

CASSIE: I don't know. At least four or five times in the last six months.

REV. BECKLEY: And now it's April fifth.

CASSIE: Right.

REV. BECKLEY: So you're staying in bed.

CASSIE: Can you think of a safer place?

REV. BECKLEY *(shrugging)*: Tell me, Cassie, you mentioned that the month on the calendar was April. Did you notice the year?

CASSIE: This year. *(Hesitates.)* At least I think it was. Why would it be a different year?

REV. BECKLEY: Beats me. It's your dream. So anyway, I take it that your conclusion is that the dream is some kind of warning that your life's in danger on this day, whatever the year.

CASSIE: I never thought about the year, but yeah, I guess that's what I think.

REV. BECKLEY: Who's warning you?

CASSIE: Huh?

REV. BECKLEY: Who's sending the dream? I mean, is there a ghost or some supernatural power at work here? Most people don't get to know in advance when they're going to die. What makes you special? You think God is sending you the dream?

CASSIE: How do I know? I guess it's possible, isn't it? Didn't God tell Joseph that Mary was a virgin by using a dream?

REV. BECKLEY: That's right, He did. But I don't think it's His preferred means of communication. Have you talked to Him about it?

CASSIE: I don't think God actually talks to anyone but television preachers and crazy people. Do you?

REV. BECKLEY (smiling): Let's just say He has a way of letting us know things. If we want to know.

CASSIE: But you don't think He'd be using my dream to do that. So I guess you think I should just get out of bed and treat this like any normal day, not paying any attention to my dream. I guess you don't believe in ESP, or clairvoyance, or any supernatural stuff like that.

REV. BECKLEY: Now, I didn't say that, and I certainly don't want to be put in the position of telling you what to do. I will say this: I'm convinced that God is perfectly aware of when you or anyone else is destined to die. I think getting out of bed today or any day is really a matter of faith, not that you're going to live, but that God is in control and that makes it okay. You can't control your fate, Cassie; nobody can.

CASSIE: That's funny, my dad says just the opposite. He wants me to get out of bed and take control of my fate.

REV. BECKLEY: Maybe we're not as far apart as it seems. We could just be looking at it differently.

CASSIE: Maybe. *(She sinks down in bed a little.)* But I think I'll still stay in bed.

REV. BECKLEY *(rising)*: Well, I guess that's your decision, Cassie. I'd just hate to see you turn into some timid little girl who's afraid to make her mark on this world.

CASSIE: That won't happen, Reverend Beckley. If I survive the day, I'll be back out there tomorrow. Thanks for coming to see me.

201

REV. BECKLEY: We wouldn't mind seeing you drop by the youth group again, either.

CASSIE: One day at a time, sir.

The REVEREND *goes out and* MRS. TATE *escorts him to the door. She returns to look in on* CASSIE.

MRS. TATE: Was that so bad?

CASSIE: He's nice, Mom. I'm just not crazy about telling people I hardly know about my psycho dreams.

MRS. TATE: Don't make jokes about it. How about some lunch?

CASSIE: And risk food poisoning? I'll pass. I think I'll take a nap. You could do me one favor. Would you listen to the weather report? I heard it's tornado season. *(Phone rings.)* Hello? Hi, Shel, what's the latest? . . . You're lying! . . . Why did he sit with you? . . . *(She waves her mother out of the room.)* Now I know you're lying. He just sits down next to you in the cafeteria and starts asking about me? Oh sure! . . . What did he want to know? . . . You're kidding! What did you tell him? . . . Omigod, you didn't! Did he believe it? He'll find out,

Shel, and then I'll have to kill you. . . . *(Long pause.)* No, I don't think so. . . . Even if I thought I could make it to school without dying, I'd feel stupid. . . . What am I supposed to say, "Hi, Tommy, I got well as soon as I heard you were asking about me"? . . . No, it'll just have to wait until tomorrow—if I last that long. . . . Yeah, come over. Thanks, Shelly. 'Bye. *(She hangs up the phone and looks at her stuffed panda.)* It would be the ultimate joke, wouldn't it, Pandy? Tommy Haffner likes me. I get the best news of my life, and then I die. You keep watch for me while I sleep, okay, Pandy?

All lights dim until the entire stage is dark. CASSIE *screams and the lights come on suddenly.*

CASSIE *(sitting up suddenly in bed)*: No! *(Leans over and grabs panda bear.)* Oh God, I hate it!

MRS. TATE *(at her door immediately)*: Cassie? Are you okay? You had it again, didn't you?

CASSIE *(nodding)*: Oh Mom, I'm so tired of this. *(She begins to cry.)*

MRS. TATE: I am too, honey. Don't you worry, you're safe here.

She sits down on the side of the bed. NEAL
comes into the room and drops his book bag
on the floor. He walks to the other side of
CASSIE'*s bed and begins taking her pulse.*

NEAL: All right! Still ticking!

CASSIE *(sarcastically)*: I didn't know you cared.

NEAL: I don't. But I bet some superstitious sucker
at school that you'd survive the day. I can make
five bucks.

MRS. TATE *(horrified)*: You're making bets about your
sister's death!

NEAL: Hey, I bet she'd live, didn't I?

CASSIE: How many people did you tell about this?

NEAL: Everybody! You're a legend at Tyler Middle
School. Don't worry, though, I covered my bet.
I bet some other guy that you wouldn't stay in
bed all day, either.

CASSIE *(spitefully)*: Well, you're gonna lose that one.
I haven't moved yet, and I'm not going to.

NEAL: Oh, sure. You haven't even gone to the bathroom?

MRS. TATE: That doesn't count.

NEAL: Does too.

CASSIE: Doesn't matter. I'm not going today.

NEAL: Oh, bull! Everyone goes to the bathroom.

CASSIE: Not today. Didn't you know most accidents in the house occur in the bathroom? I'm not taking any chances.

> *The doorbell rings.*

MRS. TATE: Go answer the door, Neal.

> SHELLY *zooms right past* NEAL *when he opens the door.*

SHELLY: Hello, dweeb. Where is she?

NEAL: In her room, savoring her last moments on earth.

SHELLY: Oh God, you too. *(She goes into the bedroom without knocking.)* Hiya, Cass. Well, you missed your big chance. Oh, hi, Mrs. Tate.

MRS. TATE: Hello, dear. What big chance is that?

SHELLY: Oh, um, nothing really. Mr. Kearn just assigned our parts to read in *Romeo and Juliet*. Since Cass was absent, she didn't get one.

MRS. TATE: Oh. Who do you get to play?

SHELLY *(proudly)*: I'm Juliet.

CASSIE *(sitting up)*: Who's Romeo?

SHELLY: Um, Tommy Haffner. Mr. Kearn kind of volunteered him.

CASSIE: Oh, great. Mom, me and Shelly need to talk, okay?

MRS. TATE: Okay, hon. I need to start fixing dinner anyway. I'm fixing your favorite.

CASSIE: Don't bother, unless I can eat it in here. And unless Neal has to taste everything first to make sure it's not poisoned.

MRS. TATE: Now what harm is it going to do for you to get up and come to the dinner table?

CASSIE *(doggedly)*: I said I wasn't getting out of bed today, and I meant it.

> MRS. TATE *shakes her head in resignation and leaves.*

CASSIE: So you're Juliet and Tommy is Romeo, huh, best friend?

SHELLY *(excitedly)*: Nah, I just made that up for your mom's benefit. He likes you, Cass, he really does.

CASSIE: What makes you so sure?

SHELLY: 'Cause he told me, dummy! After I called you at lunch, he started talking to me again. He asked me all kinds of questions about you. Cass, I told him about your dream. Is that okay?

CASSIE: What the heck. I think the whole world knows about it by now. What did he say?

SHELLY: He was really sweet about it. He acted all concerned, and he said he didn't blame you for staying home. I think he's going to ask you out.

CASSIE: Shel, if you're lying to me . . .

SHELLY: I'm not, I swear. And guess what. He even hinted he might ask you to the Sophomore Spring Formal.

CASSIE: Omigod, really? What would I do? I don't even know what I'd wear.

SHELLY: If you weren't trapped in that bed, we could

go out right now and start looking for a dress.

CASSIE *(Hesitates.)*: I think that would be jumping the gun a little, considering Tommy hasn't even talked to me. Maybe we can go to the mall tomorrow.

SHELLY: Geez, Cassie, I can't believe you! You've been talking about this guy for the last six months. Now the door pops open and you want to hide under the covers.

CASSIE: I'm not hiding under the covers. I'm just making sure I'm around when Tommy gets ready to ask me to the dance or whatever else he has in mind.

SHELLY: Cassie, I know how scary your dream is, but you can't let it paralyze your life. What happens if you have your dream again tonight? Do you worry for another year and then stay in bed again? Or what if the date on the calendar changes?

CASSIE: So what do you want me to do, Shel— pretend I don't dream?

SHELLY: No, just don't live in your dream world. I mean, what's the worst that could happen?

You go out tonight, your dream comes true, and you get smunched in a car wreck. Okay, you're dead, which is what happens to everybody anyway. In the meantime, the whole school comes to your funeral, everybody hears about your dream, your parents remember every single rotten thing they ever did to you, Tommy Haffner thinks forever of what might have been, your best friend speaks of your innermost secrets, and you become a legend. Now, is that so bad?

CASSIE: It sounds wonderful! Too bad I wouldn't be here to enjoy it.

> NEAL *comes rushing into the room looking panic-stricken.*

NEAL: Fire! The upstairs is in flames! Quick, we have to get out of here! *(He runs to the bed and grabs* CASSIE's *arm.* SHELLY *has already jumped up from the bed and is looking around frantically.)*

SHELLY: My purse! Where's my purse?

CASSIE *(calmly)*: I'm not going anywhere.

SHELLY: Cassie! This could be the dream!

CASSIE: The day I let this little con man run my life is the day I'm ready to hang it up.

NEAL: Damn! I thought sure I'd get ya on that one.

> MR. TATE *sticks his head into* CASSIE'*s bedroom*.

MR. TATE: Hello, gang. What's all the ruckus?

CASSIE: Didn't you hear, Dad? The house is burning down.

MR. TATE: Well, no one seems very worried about it. Hello, Shelly. I see you haven't managed to get my daughter out of bed.

SHELLY: Not that I haven't tried, Mr. Tate.

NEAL: Tell her she has to get out, Dad.

MR. TATE *(regarding* CASSIE *thoughtfully)*: No, I'm not going to do that. I wouldn't mind talking about it a little more, though.

CASSIE: That's okay with me.

SHELLY *(edging toward the door)*: Well, I sure need to get going, I know that. You take care, okay, Cass? I'll see you tomorrow.

CASSIE: I hope so.

NEAL: I guess I'll clear out, too. Unless Mom's planning on serving dinner in here.

SHELLY *exits and* NEAL *seems to disappear.*

MR. TATE: So, how are you feeling?

CASSIE: Okay. So far, so good.

MR. TATE: I'm glad. I've been thinking a lot about you today.

CASSIE: Have you?

MR. TATE: Of course. All day long I've felt like I was a little hard on you this morning, like you might think I didn't take you seriously, or, even worse, that I didn't really care. I know that showing affection doesn't come real easy to me, but nothing could be further from the truth. I want you to know that if I thought for one minute that your life was in danger, I'd do anything I could to make sure you were safe. And I sure can't claim to be an expert on dreams and ESP and stuff like that. So maybe you have the right idea, sitting in bed and waiting for a day like this to be over. But I'll tell you what bothers me. Every day in my work, I see people who always manage, for one reason or another, to find an excuse for being less than what they should be. These people are usually unhappy, and it's never their own fault. They don't like their jobs, if they have them, and their families don't understand them, and they take no notice of the simple pleasures that life affords. In fact, they don't see much of anything beyond their own lives. And I think I've noticed one common characteristic that all those people like that share—they're afraid. Their fear keeps them from taking ahold of life and making something out of it. I don't want that to happen to you.

CASSIE: Don't worry, Dad. As soon as I make it through this day, I'll be out there like gangbusters. I promise.

MR. TATE: I hope so, honey. (*A little awkwardly, he bends over and kisses her forehead.*) I guess you ought to, uh, rest up for it then. (*He exits.*)

CASSIE (*to the panda bear*): Well, Pandy, I'm starting to think we're going to make it. Boy, I can't remember the last time Daddy talked to me like that. For staying in bed all day, we sure have had a lot of company. I don't know anymore if staying in bed was the right idea, but I do know I'm glad to be alive.

The doorbell rings. MRS. TATE *opens it and invites in an extremely handsome teenage boy. She talks with him briefly, then crosses the floor to* CASSIE's *room.*

MRS. TATE: Cassie, there's a boy from school here. He says he brought you some assignments, and he was hoping he could talk with you. *(She hesitates.)* Shall I have him come to your room? His name is Tommy.

CASSIE *(practically leaping out of bed)*: No way, Mom! Are you crazy? You go out and stall him somehow. Omigod, look at my hair. And what should I wear? Quick, what did he have on? Shorts? T-shirt or buttoned shirt? Never mind. Go, go!

> MRS. TATE *returns to living room while* CASSIE *buzzes around like a madwoman. In a very short time she looks presentable. Her room is a shambles, and poor Pandy is lying on the floor.* CASSIE *stops at the door, takes a deep breath, and makes her entrance. She moves across stage to* TOMMY, *and they begin talking*

animatedly. Then NEAL *slowly crawls out from under* CASSIE's *bed, looks around, and raises his hands triumphantly toward the ceiling.*

NEAL: Thank you, God, thank you!

CURTAIN

DALLIN MALMGREN

Born in Albany, New York, Dallin Malmgren was graduated from the University of Missouri–Columbia in 1981 and has been teaching English and journalism ever since, the last six years in Converse, Texas. He says, "I have wanted to be a writer since the seventh grade, when I got a D for using a cuss word in a short story I wrote." In his first novel, *The Whole Nine Yards*, a young man, obsessed with girls and seeking excitement in dangerous activities, eventually faces death and learns what love is all about.

Malmgren's second novel, *The Ninth Issue*, follows the staff of a high school newspaper who, along with their journalism teacher, change a boring school newspaper into a prize-winning publication that raises serious issues about school activities.

Other than being a voracious reader and helping to critique some of the high school plays where he teaches, Dallin Malmgren had had no personal theater experiences. "Since I would never have the courage to stand up on a stage and act, I have tremendous respect for people who do," he confesses. *Large Fears, Little Demons* is his first attempt at writing a play, an activity he asserts was very enjoyable. The idea for the play came from a disturbing dream that a girl in one of his classes had. On the day designated in her dream for her to die, she was absent from school, Malmgren noted. Although it turned out that she had a scheduled doctor's appointment, Malmgren's imagination had already taken over.

HUM IT AGAIN, JEREMY

by Jean Davies Okimoto

CHARACTERS

JEREMY BOTKIN, a young man about sixteen

ROSALIE BOTKIN, his mother

DAN BOTKIN, his father

DARRELL WASHINGTON, Jeremy's best friend

SETTING

TIME: *An evening in May.*

PLACE: *Cleveland, Ohio.*

An asphalt basketball court on a dimly lit play-ground, center stage, in front of an apartment building. It is littered with cans and papers. There is one streetlight above the hoop. As the curtain rises, we see DARRELL WASHINGTON, *a sixteen-year-old young man dressed in jeans and a T-shirt, shooting baskets alone on the court. It is eight o'clock.*

DARRELL: ~~Where you been, man?~~ *(Irritated, he pivots and makes a sharp chest shot to* JEREMY BOTKIN, *who bursts on the court, out of breath. He is a tall, gangly sixteen-year-old, dressed in jeans and a Cleveland Cavaliers T-shirt.)*

JEREMY *(Catches ball, jarred backward a bit by its unexpected force. He tucks ball under his arm and makes "time out" signal.):* Time. *(He throws ball underarm like a referee to* DARRELL.*)* *not so sudden*

DARRELL *(accusingly):* ~~It's dark.~~

JEREMY *(holding hands up, shaking his head):* Not you too—I can't handle it.

DARRELL *(Pauses, irritated. He looks around the court, dribbling the ball hard. Then sighs, resignedly.):* Okay. *(He bounces the ball once, catches it, and pauses again.)*Let's play. *Keep*

JEREMY *(guarding* DARRELL, *who dribbles toward basket):* *Do, but* Thanks for ~~waiting.~~ *Staying* *(*DARRELL *shoots, guarded by* JEREMY, *then* JEREMY *shoots, guarded by* DARRELL. DARRELL *shoots, guarded by* JEREMY.*):* ~~Nice shot.~~ *[Substitute* ~~"Almost . . . nice shot"~~ *if ball* ~~doesn't go in.]~~

219

DARRELL (*guarding* JEREMY, *who takes shot*): I figured it was your mom, your old man, or Renee.

JEREMY: All of the above. (*Guards* DARRELL, *who shoots. He gets* DARRELL's *rebound, then shoots and misses, and* DARRELL *gets the ball.*)

DARRELL: It's the Jam Man. (*Dribbles to basket, goes up, and slam dunks in the air a foot below the basket.* JEREMY *cracks up at the air dunk.* DARRELL *passes to* JEREMY.)

JEREMY (*dribbling toward basket as* DARRELL *guards*): You know what would be great?

DARRELL (*guarding* JEREMY): What?

JEREMY (*Shoots, catches his own rebound, and dribbles ball in place.*): If you could do a trade. In your family—like it was a team. I'd get a power father. My present one doesn't come to play—as they say. (*Passes ball to* DARRELL.) So I'd just trade him.

DARRELL (*dribbling toward basket as* JEREMY *guards*): For money? Or another player?

JEREMY: My mom would want the money. She's into the green. It's all she talks about, but this is my deal, see? I'd trade him for another player. (*Shooting*) I'd trade him for Bill Cosby.

DARRELL (*shouting excitedly*): All right, My mom for
~~Tina Turner!~~ *more!*
Madonna *chant*

JEREMY (*bending down to tie his shoe*): That's not the
idea, man. You never see ~~Tina Turner~~ *Madonna* with kids
or anything like that. See—you scout a different
kind of talent for this trade. Like, take Bill Cosby.
Everyone knows he loves his kids—

DARRELL (*holding ball, snapping fingers and singing Tina
~~Turner~~ song*): "~~What's love got to do, got to do
with it?~~" *love justify my love.*

JEREMY (*Stands up, takes ball from* DARRELL. *Flatly*):
Sometimes—I wonder. (*Dribbles toward basket.
Freezes as set becomes black.*) *Stand & stare*

Earlier the same day.
Spots light the living room of the Botkin apart-
ment, which is set on risers on the left of the
stage. Furnished with a worn couch and match-
ing chair, it is a small L-shaped room with a
formica dinette set in the end of the room next
to the adjoining small kitchen, which is offstage.
On an end table next to the chair is a phone
with a long extension cord that can reach
around the corner to the kitchen offstage. An
exercise bike is in the corner of the room facing

Lights fade down with light faint on Jeremy light fade up with mother screaming

221

a television set. Over the television is a macramé wall hanging, and on the wall behind the dinette set is a plate commemorating the wedding of Prince Charles and Princess Di. There is a large plant in the corner of the living room, many of its leaves brown and dying. On the formica coffee table in front of the sofa is an arrangement of plastic flowers and a Walkman radio. ROSALIE BOTKIN *is riding the exercise bike and watching the shopping channel on TV. She is a short, chunky woman with obviously dyed auburn hair. Dressed in pink sweats, she is scowling and puffing as she pedals the bike.*

ROSALIE *(shouting)*: Jeremy! Don't leave this apartment without talking to me. *(She pedals laboriously and begins to pant before shouting again, louder.)* I have to talk to you, Jeremy. *(*JEREMY *enters, leans against top of easy chair, holding car keys.)*

JEREMY: I gotta go, Mom. After I have dinner with him—I'm supposed to meet Darrell. *(Heads for the door.)*

ROSALIE: Just tell him to give me the check. *(She runs a hand through her hair, then wipes her forearm across her brow.)* I want that check, Jeremy. *(Carefully, she gets off the bike rubbing her thighs, then slowly goes to the chair and flops down in it as the phone rings.)* Stay right here—I'm not through. *(While* ROSALIE *answers the phone,* JEREMY *dribbles and shoots an imaginary basketball.)* Hello. . . . Yeah, he's here. *(Covering the mouthpiece)* It's that girl. Why don't you bring her to meet me? She's forward enough to call you, she ought to meet your mother. *(She hands the phone to* JEREMY.*)* Here.

JEREMY *(taking the phone, angrily mouthing)*: Shhhhhh. *(He disappears into the kitchen around the corner with the phone.)*

ROSALIE *(nagging, as* JEREMY *disappears to kitchen)*: And if you want to know, I still don't think it's right for girls to be calling boys. *(She lies on the floor, begins doing sit-ups; after four sit-ups* JEREMY *enters and heads for door. She sits up.)* You were the one card I had, Jeremy. If he didn't pay—I wouldn't let him see you. So—now you're driving a car, you're a big guy, you go see the jerk whenever you please. You think we don't need the money or something? Don't you give a damn about my feelings?

JEREMY *(impatiently, jiggling the car keys)*: Listen Mom—

ROSALIE: No, you listen! Because of you I don't have any control over this situation. Not unless I want to go to some lawyer, and those greedy slobs won't even talk to me unless I give 'em a hundred bucks up front. Now if I had an extra hundred bucks lying around, I wouldn't need a lawyer, would I?

JEREMY *(nodding, defeatedly)*: Yeah, Mom. *(Quietly, mumbling)* Yeah.

ROSALIE *(softening)*: Look, this is strictly business. Why can't you see that you're the only leverage I've got? I'm not trying to make you hate him, Jeremy.

JEREMY: You know . . . *(He pauses, leaning back against door.)* It's beyond me how the two of you ever got together.

ROSALIE *(quietly, shaking her head)*: You aren't the only one to wonder that.

JEREMY: What d'you mean, Mom?

ROSALIE *(Stands and gets on exercise bike.)*: Oh—just

that no one ever looked at me. I was just known as Elaine's kid sister. *(Starts pedaling.)* So when Dan Botkin came around for me, I thought it was a mistake. And then—when he actually wanted to marry me—me, Rosalie—well . . . *(She pauses.)* I thought I'd died and gone to heaven.

JEREMY: Some heaven.

ROSALIE *(bitterly)*: Yeah. Some heaven. I shoulda known better. Like ya been told, your grandfather was a drunk—just as well you didn't know that bum—but your father didn't touch the stuff— and that impressed me. In fact, I thought I was the luckiest girl on the block. *(Sighs.)* But for all the good he did us, he might as well've been a drunk like his old man. Dan's great disappearing act. Now you see him—now you don't. When I think about it, the only thing he ever did for me *(pausing)* was for one brief moment in my life *(pausing again, leaning forward on handlebars)* he made me feel beautiful. *(She shakes her head, starts pedaling.)* I guess that's something.

JEREMY *(embarrassed)*: I gotta go, Mom.

ROSALIE *(fiercely)*: Jeremy, you tell your father that if he doesn't come up with that check, I got a lawyer who'll call his lines and garnish his pay. You tell him that, Jeremy!

JEREMY: See you later, Mom. *(Turns toward door.)*

ROSALIE *(Stops pedaling. Tenderly, as* JEREMY *exits)*: Drive carefully, Jeremy. *(Gets off bike, goes to door and shouts after him.)* Jeremy! You damn well better come back here with that check! *and I want to meet that girl*

Blacking out

Set becomes black.
Lights come back up on basketball court. JEREMY *and* DARRELL *are sitting on the ground leaning back against the apartment wall that borders the court.*

JEREMY: You see the Cavs last night?

DARRELL: A little, before I had to go to work. They didn't look that bad in the first quarter.

JEREMY: They sure blew it in the fourth. It was pitiful. I shoulda gone over to Renee's instead of watching 'em. I oughta give up on those clowns.

DARRELL: How's Renee?

JEREMY *(depressed)*: Mr. Sanduzi wouldn't let me see her.

226

DARRELL: That's cold.

JEREMY *(sarcastically)*: Yeah. Tell me about it. *(He stands and bounces the ball.)* I stop by her apartment on my way to see my dad. She'd even called and asked me to come by. So I get there, I buzz their apartment, and Mr. Sanduzi comes on the intercom. He says *(mimicking a low growling voice)* "Renee's got to help her mother, Botkin. Don't come up here." *(He passes the ball to* DARRELL, *who stands in place and dribbles it.* JEREMY *picks up a can and throws it against the brick wall of the apartment building.)*

DARRELL: It was bad with your dad too—huh?

JEREMY: Yeah. Like I said—he doesn't come to play.

Set darkens.
Earlier that evening:
Spots light DAN BOTKIN's *apartment bedroom, which is set on risers on the right of stage. It is furnished with a double bed, a dresser, a chair, and an end table that holds a phone and a lamp. A closet is across from the bed; next to the chair is a window. The furnishings are sparse and cheap in contrast to the appearance of* DAN BOTKIN, *a balding, middle-aged man;*

he is a sharp dresser, wearing a silk sport coat.
He has several large gold rings on his fingers.
DAN is packing his suitcase while JEREMY stands
by the window, looking out.

DAN *(cheerily)*: Who d'ya think'll make the playoffs, Jeremy?

JEREMY *(looking out the window, turning away from DAN)*: I dunno.

DAN: Sonics are looking good.

JEREMY *(sadly)*: Yeah.

DAN: Bullets have a shot. *(Chuckles.)* Little joke there, Jeremy. *(He pauses, waiting for a response from JEREMY, who silently stares out the window.)* Hey— not even a courtesy laugh?

JEREMY: I don't feel like laughing.

DAN: Look—I told you I was sorry about tonight. We'll do it some other time.

JEREMY *(mumbling, voice fading)*: Like always—

DAN: What? Speak up, wouldya?

JEREMY *(shouting)*: It's always some other time!

DAN: Listen, kid. You don't have it so bad. Name one time I ever laid a hand on you, Jeremy.

JEREMY *(expressionless)*: You never laid a hand on me, Dad.

DAN: See this watch? Read that name. R-O-L-E-X. Best watch money can buy, and I earned every damn dime to pay for it. My old man couldn't blink at a watch like this. You know, Jeremy— when I wear this watch *(pausing)* I feel like some- body. It's insurance, too. I've never had to—but if I ever got in a jam—it's liquid—instant cash. But so far *(knocking on dresser)* the Lord willin' and the river don't rise—I've never had to.

JEREMY *(coldly)*: Mom says she needs the check.

DAN *(defensively)*: Look, Jeremy, my lines aren't pay- ing me. They're slime. Take it from me, don't ever be a rep in the rag business—it's not worth it. They're supposed to pay me next week. *(Angrily, slamming suitcase shut)* Tell your mother I'm doing the best I can.

JEREMY: When'll you be back?

DAN: This week I've got Akron, Salem, Columbus, and Cincinnati. Probably the end of the week—

but I know a gal in Cincinnati, so—might be the first of next if I get lucky. She's pretty—but I got my eyes open. You can't trust pretty women. You want one that'll stick around. I'm sure what led my old man to the bottle was when my mother took off. *(Lifts suitcase off bed.)* You know, the only thing I remember about her is bright-red lips and she smelled like cigarettes and soap. Funny, huh?

JEREMY: Yeah. not really

DAN: And a little song she used to sing. Only you know what, Jeremy?

JEREMY *(sadly)*: What?

DAN: I even forgot the song. *(Gets trench coat from the closet.)* So—tell your mother—next week. *(Takes out wallet and hands* JEREMY *a five-dollar bill.)* Sorry about dinner. Get yourself something to eat with this, okay?

JEREMY *(taking bill, looking at floor)*: Can I see you next week?

DAN: Sure kid—I'll call you.

> Set becomes black.
> Scenes alternate among the basketball court,

230

JEREMY's *apartment, and* DAN BOTKIN's *apartment.*

JEREMY *(holding ball under his arm)*: Beats me why I don't give up on the jerk.

DARRELL *(shrugging)*: Maybe for the same reason we don't give up on the Cavs.

JEREMY: Yeah. Every season we think this'll be the year they put it all together. *(Pauses.)* You know— sometimes I feel like this damn ball.

Bounces ball four times. Set becomes black. Spot on stage left.

ROSALIE *(rapidly)*: Tell your father—

Ball bounces once, punctuating. Spot on stage right.

DAN: Tell your mother—

Ball bounces once. Spot on stage left.

ROSALIE: Tell your father—

Ball bounces once. Spot on stage right.

DAN: Tell your mother—

Ball bounces once. Spot on stage left.

ROSALIE: Tell your father—

Ball bounces once. Spot on stage right.

DAN: Tell your mother—

Ball bounces once. Set darkens. Spot on basketball court.

DARRELL (*dribbling toward basket as* JEREMY *guards*): Who was the greatest forward?

JEREMY (*going up for rebound and getting it*): All-time?

DARRELL (*guarding* JEREMY): All-time.

JEREMY (*shooting*): Elgin Baylor.

DARRELL (*getting rebound as* JEREMY *guards him*): The Bird Man.

JEREMY (*Catches ball that* DARRELL *passes to him. They pass it back and forth, taking a break from the game.*): The greatest guard?

DARRELL: Magic.

JEREMY: Michael Jordan.

DARRELL: Jerry West.

JEREMY: Oscar Robertson.

DARRELL: Gail Goodrich. *(Dribbles toward basket and shoots, as* JEREMY *guards.)*

JEREMY *(Getting rebound, takes ball out and shoots, while* DARRELL *guards.)*: Center?

DARRELL *(Bounce passes to* JEREMY, *who returns it as they punctuate each player they name with a pass.)*: Kareem.

JEREMY: Bill Russell.

DARRELL: Wilt Chamberlain.

JEREMY: Akeem Olajuwon.

DARRELL: Soon to be the greatest?

JEREMY: Mark Eaton. *(Dribbles the ball toward basket. Stops. There is a pause as he holds ball and looks straight at* DARRELL.) Know who I'd like to be?

DARRELL *(standing under basket, leaning against pole)*: Who, man?

JEREMY *(quietly)*: Denny.

DARRELL: Denny? Who—Denny Crum? Coach at Louisville?

JEREMY *(Bounces ball once, then holds it again.)*: Nope.

DARRELL: You mean baseball? That Tigers pitcher Denny McClain?

JEREMY (*Walks across court and sits down, leaning back against the brick wall of the apartment building.*): Denny. The guy that owns all those restaurants. Makes people happy. You know, Denny's. It's open all night. All day. You can get pancakes and stuff—everybody likes to go there. That Denny.

DARRELL (*Walks to edge of court.* JEREMY *tosses him the ball. He sits down next to* JEREMY.): Yeah. That'd be nice.

JEREMY: You know who else I'd like to be?

DARRELL: Ronald McDonald?

JEREMY: No, man. The guy at the games, all the games—basketball, football, baseball—you name it. The guy that plays "The Star-Spangled Banner."

DARRELL: You serious? How come you wanna be that guy?

JEREMY: Because when he plays that song, all the people in the whole place stand up. All he does is play that one song, and all those thousands of people stand up. God, I think that'd be so great.

Set becomes black.

The Botkin apartment. Nine thirty the same night. JEREMY *is sitting at the table near the kitchen, eating a sandwich and drinking a glass of milk.*

ROSALIE *(Enters through door off living room. She is dressed in a faded bathrobe and is rubbing cream on her face.)*: I thought you had dinner. *(She sits across from him at the table.)*

JEREMY *(not looking at her, taking a bite of the sandwich)*: He had to—

ROSALIE *(interrupting him)*: Don't talk with your mouth full, Jeremy.

JEREMY *(Slowly chews sandwich. Takes a gulp of milk. Wipes his arm across his mouth.)*: We didn't have dinner. He had to leave. *(Continues to finish eating sandwich.)*

ROSALIE *(angrily)*: Typical. *(She leans back and folds her arms across her chest and glares at him. Demandingly)* Did you get the check? *(JEREMY picks up empty plate and glass and goes to kitchen. ROSALIE stands up and calls after him.)* I gotta have that check, Jeremy!

JEREMY *(Returns from kitchen, opens wallet, and takes out*

five-dollar bill and hands it to ROSALIE.*)*: He gave me this.

ROSALIE *(Grabs money, holds out bill, and looks at it disgustedly.)*: That's all you came back with? *(Stares at bill, then stuffs it in her bathrobe pocket and crosses room to door.* JEREMY *stands, holding back of chair looking helpless. She calls over her shoulder, before exit to bedroom.)* You're as worthless as he is!

> *Lights dim.* JEREMY *sits at table. One elbow is on the table and he props his forehead against his hand. He sits like this for a minute, then gets up and goes to the living room and grabs his Walkman from the coffee table. He puts on the earphones, fiddles with the dial, and returns to the kitchen. He sits again, leaning forward, elbows on the table, with his chin propped in his hands. After a few minutes he takes off the earphones and goes to the kitchen. He disappears for a minute, then returns holding phone, pulling cord, and leaning against the kitchen wall. Set darkens. A spot is on* JEREMY. *At the end of the stage another spot is on* DARRELL, *sitting in a chair, holding a phone.*

JEREMY: Darrell?

DARRELL: Hi, man. How's it goin'?

JEREMY *(pausing a moment, then, defeatedly)*: It's air balls—my life's just air balls. *(A pause. Hopelessly)* Nothing I do goes in.

DARRELL *(not really understanding)*: Hmmm.

JEREMY *(flatly)*: Mr. Sanduzi won't let me near Renee. My dad gives me five bucks and splits. I give it to my mom. She tells me I'm as worthless as he is. *(A pause. He pounds his thigh. Turns toward wall.)* Sometimes—some . . . *(His voice catches.)*

DARRELL: Jeremy?

JEREMY *(Holding phone, he leans his forehead against the wall, his back to the audience. His shoulders shake as he begins to cry quietly. After a few minutes, he takes a deep breath and wipes the back of his hand across his eyes. A long pause. Quietly)*: Sometimes I just wanna go to Lake Erie and walk off in the water. It'd be so cold, you'd just feel nothing. Just close your eyes and the water'd come all around and it'd be cold and you'd just feel nothing. *(A long silence.)*

DARRELL: Hum, Jeremy.

JEREMY: What?

DARRELL: I said hum, man. Hum "The Star-Spangled Banner." *(A pause. Forcefully)* DO IT, MAN!
JUST DO IT!

Hesitantly, JEREMY *starts to hum the first few
bars of "The Star-Spangled Banner," then
stops, then starts again.*

DARRELL *(Stands up.)*: I'm standing up, Jeremy. (JER-
EMY *stops humming, half smiles.)* Hum it again, Jeremy. I'm standing up. (JEREMY *hums as the light dims
and the curtain drops slowly.)*

CURTAIN

JEAN DAVIES OKIMOTO

Before she started writing books for young people, Jean Davies Okimoto was a remedial reading tutor in a high school and then an assistant to the director of a youth services bureau.

Her novels for young people include *My Mother Is Not Married to My Father* and its sequel, *It's Just Too Much*. Both deal with divorce and remarriage. *Norman Schnurman, Average Person* also focuses on family problems. *Who Did It, Jenny Lake?* is a teenage murder mystery, and *Jason's Women* was an American Library Association Best Book for Young Adults.

Jean Okimoto is also a book reviewer of self-help books for the *Seattle Times*, and is coauthor of the nonfiction *Boomerang Kids: How to Live with Adult Children Who Return Home*. She has just published her first picture book for children, *Blumpoe the Grumpo Meets Arnold the Cat*—about a cat that lives in a country inn with eighteen other cats. She is also completing two other novels, one called *Molly By Any Other Name*, the other *Take a Chance, Gramps!*

She concocted skits when she was in high school, created material for a variety show at Fairchild Air Force Base, wrote a short play, which was performed on the radio, for the Seattle Human Relations Council, and has been working on several screenplays. *Hum It Again, Jeremy* is Jean Okimoto's first published play.

In addition to writing, Jean Davies Okimoto works as a psychotherapist in private practice in Seattle, Washington.

HOLDING OUT

by Ouida Sebestyen

CHARACTERS

CURTIS

VALERIE

INDIANS OF THE MODOC TRIBE

SETTING

TIME: *The present, late afternoon on a chilly spring day.*
A roadside rest area. One sturdy picnic table with benches and a trash can are the only signs of civilization. Behind them, in dimmer light, jagged outcroppings of lava rock and clumps of sagebrush stair-step up a desolate slope. A drum is beating softly, almost like the thump of a heart.

AT CURTAIN RISE: CURTIS *strides out among the rocks at right. He is sixteen, and comfortable being alone. He stumbles on a stone and pushes it out of the trail with a slender branch he is using as a staff. He also carries the thin National Park Service booklet he has used on a self-guided hike. He looks around and, because no one is there to see, holds it with his teeth so he can pretend his staff is a rifle. After a few quick shots he climbs up on the table and continues to read, deeply interested. A truck door slams. He stiffens. A few moments later* VALERIE *appears, dressed like him in jeans and sweatshirt, raking her tangled hair. Neither of them takes notice of the drum, which slowly fades away.*

VALERIE: Curtis, don't *do* stuff like this to me. I woke up and there I was, parked all by myself in the middle of nowhere, with my feet out the window.

CURTIS *(pointing up the slope)*: There's a trail up there that makes a loop. So I walked around it, to get the kinks out.

VALERIE: Yeah, tell me about kinks. I feel like the Hunchback of Notre Dame. How long did I sleep?

CURTIS: About six hours.

VALERIE: You're kidding. Nobody can sleep six hours in the cab of a pickup truck and live to tell about it.

CURTIS: Well, I guess you just made medical history.

VALERIE: Where *is* this? Are we still in Oregon?

CURTIS *(taking a pebble out of his shoe)*: No, we've crossed back into California. After you didn't wake up, I thought, What am I supposed to be doing? So I pulled off the highway and stopped here.

VALERIE: Oh, man—no. Not back in California.

CURTIS: What was I supposed to do, with you zonked out? Turn west and drive till we went down in the Pacific, blub, blub, blub?

VALERIE: You could have waked me up, for starters.

CURTIS *(softening)*: I guess. But you'd done nearly all the driving last night, and you looked really pooped. Snoring away like that. I sort of—

VALERIE: I wasn't tired from last night. I was tired from this morning.

CURTIS: Yeah, I know. I saw it. When you came out of your dad's house, you looked really different. Your face was white. I thought maybe he'd hit you, or something, and that's why you wouldn't say anything when I tried to talk.

VALERIE: No, I just had to—I don't know—get into

a little dark space and stay really quiet for a while. Curled up. Like a snail. And just wait till the shock wore off. Okay?

CURTIS: Hey, you don't have to explain it. I just didn't know what to do. So I just kept on driving and thinking and wondering. One spot up there in the mountains I was screaming along through this snowstorm. In my dad's truck. Oh, man. I never drove in a snowstorm before. So I thought I better stop, for Pete's sake, and hang around here till you joined the world again.

VALERIE *(looking around)*: You didn't pick a really great spot, Curt. This is pretty awful.

CURTIS: I don't know—it's kind of interesting. All this dark-red jagged rock is hardened lava. You know, like Hawaii.

VALERIE: It figures: I go to sleep in a truck and wake up in a lava bed. Couldn't you have stopped in a town? What am I supposed to do for a rest room?

CURTIS: There's one up the trail. Over past that dark bunch of junipers.

VALERIE: Oh, great. It would be. *(She takes a few uncertain steps that bring her back to her starting point.)*

Did you read the same thing I did about some kidnaper or hired killer or somebody—

CURTIS: Oh, that? Yeah—he dumped the body in one of these pits. Not out in the bushes where nobody ever goes—no, it's got to be in there where some Park Service guy can notice it. But I guess maybe he was thinking the quicklime or whatever would dissolve the—

VALERIE: Curtis! Shut up. Just shut up—you're gross. I'm not in any shape for scary stories. Or this weirdo place, whatever it is.

CURTIS: It's a national monument. So don't put it down—the government's trying hard to keep weirdo places like this unspoiled for our grandchildren. *(He rethinks.)* Well, not *our* grandchildren . . .

VALERIE: So where is everybody?

CURTIS: I guess March is still off season. There's maybe some kind of visitors' center, farther up the road. But it's probably closed. So people just drive through, like us.

VALERIE: No store, or anything? What do we eat?

CURTIS: We've still got the apples. And potato chips.
I can go see what else.

VALERIE *(uneasily)*:   Okay. And I guess I can go see
if anybody is stashed in the outhouse. *(She starts
off again, and turns back.)* Curtis, if I yell, you better
come running.

CURTIS: Don't I always? *(His question stops her, and
they lock eyes. She jerks around and goes up left among
the looming lava shapes. He goes off to the parked truck.)*

A MODOC INDIAN SENTRY *stands up unhur-
riedly from behind a rock and watches them
go. Another* SENTRY *rises from his nearby hiding place. They wear simple rough shirts and
pants, and round flat-brimmed hats decorated
with feathers. Their faces and hands, their
clothing and moccasins, their cartridge belts and
long 1870's rifles, are shades of gray, as if
they were being seen through gauze, or the
haze of time. They study the horizon carefully,
pointing and nodding to each other. Their
movements are slow, almost trancelike with fa-
tigue. They watch with quiet interest as* CURTIS
*returns and puts two paper sacks and a can of
pop on the table. His gaze goes past them and*

he starts to read. VALERIE *comes back and walks past them, unaware.*

VALERIE: Yuck. Can't they design those things to flush or something? *(She is holding a large feather, which she sticks into her hair.)* Boy, talk about primitive.

CURTIS: Beats a bush.

VALERIE: Just barely.

CURTIS *(noticing the feather)*: What's that?

VALERIE: I found it. Some critter got ambushed, I reckon. Oh, great, you found something to drink.

CURTIS: If you don't mind drinking from the same can.

VALERIE: You're really cute, Curt. Here we are, runaways, with a practically stolen truck on our hands, and maybe the police hunting us by now. And your folks yelling, "Where's our baby boy!" And my mom blaming everybody in sight—and you make it sound like we're on a shy little first date. *(She drinks and hands him the can.)* Hey, you found the cookies. I forgot we saved some. *(She divvies them up.)* I'm starved! Aren't you?

CURTIS (*gently nudging her toward reality*):   Valerie, this is all the food we've got. And we're running low on gas. We need to talk about what we're doing.

VALERIE: We know what we're doing. We're having a picnic in lava land. (*She starts to eat an apple from one of the sacks.*)

CURTIS: No, what we're doing is putting off talking about what happened. And what we're going to do *now*. What direction we're going.

VALERIE: Curtis, give me a break. I'm not ready. It's too soon—it's just too— Eat. Okay?

CURTIS (*regretfully*):   Val, your dad doesn't want you. You've got to go back home.

VALERIE: Back home? What home? (*She forces an airy laugh.*) You mean my mom's apartment, where I hang my clothes and step over the bottles? That home?

CURTIS: Whatever you call it, it's the only place you've got to live in.

VALERIE: That's a big lie. I've got the whole world to live in. I can live right here. People live in trucks.

CURTIS: Not in my dad's truck, they don't.

VALERIE: I can get a job and have my own apartment.

CURTIS: On that twenty-five bucks you've got left?

VALERIE: I've got money. I've got another forty I didn't tell you about.

CURTIS: Yeah? Forty that sort of stuck to your fingers while your mom wasn't looking?

VALERIE: Forty I saved! *(She tests other answers.)* I found it. My dad sent it for my birthday.

CURTIS: Okay. Forget it.

VALERIE: If you're in such a hurry to back out, why don't you just get in your daddy's precious pickup and drive off? I don't need this.

CURTIS: Sure you don't. But you needed *me*, Val. You needed the stupid truck to get to Oregon and find your dad, so I took it and got you there. You call that backing out?

VALERIE: Okay! *(She slings an apple core away, just missing him.)* I needed you. I used you. Sue me.

CURTIS: Val—I'm not mad at you! I'm just telling

you something. Your dad's not going to take you in. *(He picks up her apple core and puts it in the trash can.)* Listen, you don't have to talk about it till you're ready. But you've got to rethink your plans now. It's not going to be the way you were dreaming it. *(She begins to pace rapidly.)* What are you doing?

VALERIE: Exercising. *(She marches up and down, swinging her arms.* CURTIS *and the* MODOC SENTRIES *watch, bemused.)* I'm stiff. I hurt.

CURTIS: Why don't you walk around the trail loop? It's just about half a mile.

VALERIE: Because I want to walk around right here. Okay?

CURTIS: Sure. Forget it. *(He returns to his booklet, refusing to look at her.)*

An OLD WOMAN *in a shawl and long skirt, gray with time, enters right and brings a small jug to the two* SENTRIES. *They drink sparingly. When she offers the jug again, they shake their heads and go back to their lookout posts. She hobbles off, left, perhaps to others. Neither* CURTIS *nor* VALERIE *take notice.*

VALERIE *(looking around, still angry but curious)*:   What's the trail for, anyway? What's up there? It's just flat.

CURTIS: That's what's strange. It looks like a plain old pasture full of sagebrush. From here you can't tell that the lava is all broken up into crevices and ledges and little caves. It's like World War One up there. Full of trenches.

VALERIE: That book's telling about it?

CURTIS: Yeah. They have them up there in a little box by the trail so you can take a self-guided walk.

VALERIE: Trust you to find a book to stick your nose into, even out here in no-man's-land.

CURTIS: There were people here, once. There were some Indians called Modocs, and they had a war here. Well, more like a siege, I guess you'd say, because about sixty men held off the United States Army for months, holed up in those crevices.

VALERIE *(forgetting to pace)*:   What for?

CURTIS: Because all this around here was their homeland. But the white settlers wanted it, and

got the government to send the Modocs to live
on a reservation with another tribe they didn't
like. So they ran away, and when the Army or-
dered them back, they refused, and gathered up
their people here in the lava beds to hold out.

VALERIE: You mean women and little kids and
everybody?

CURTIS: Yeah, the old folks. The horses and dogs.
Everything they had.

VALERIE: What did they eat?

CURTIS *(with a shrug)*: What they could find, I guess.
And there's a lake back over there. They sneaked
down to it at first, but toward the last the soldiers
cut off their water supply.

> VALERIE *starts to drink the last of the pop,
> but hesitates, and impulsively offers it to* CUR-
> TIS. *He shakes his head. She drinks thought-
> fully, looking around.*

VALERIE: Why the blazes didn't the Army just let
them *have* their stupid hunk of land and save everybody a lot of trouble?

> *As she speaks, the two* SENTRIES *stand up warily
> as a small tattered group of* MODOC MEN *and*

WOMEN *gathers between them. Two tall im-*
posing men are obviously rival leaders, unable
to agree about something. They mime an ar-
gument. Their supporters, anxiously watching,
slowly divide into separate sides.

CURTIS: Yeah, that's what some people back east
wondered. *(He waves the booklet, which has given him*
the story.) So finally they sent out five people to
be, like, a peace committee or something, to try
to talk.

The FIRST LEADER *defends his position pas-*
sionately, but the SECOND LEADER *senses*
weakness in him, and suddenly grabs a woman's
shawl and drapes it over his rival's head. The
FIRST LEADER, *shocked, throws it off, but he*
has been called a coward. His followers back
away from him.

CURTIS: But it turned out the Modocs had broken
up into two groups with two chiefs. One chief
kept trying to work things out. But the other
groups just—stood up at a meeting and blew away
a general and a minister from the peace party.
Naturally the Army said, "That does it—not a
general," and started lobbing mortar shells into the

hideout every fifteen minutes. Like, this is *war*, man—no more shilly-shally stuff.

In deep anguish the FIRST LEADER *reluctantly agrees with the* SECOND, *who hurries off triumphantly with his men. The little gray crowd melts away. In sharp contrast to* CURTIS's *flippant comment, the* FIRST LEADER *sinks to his knees in despair.*

VALERIE (*rubbing her shoulders*): It's cold here. The sun's about to go down, isn't it? How do you suppose they stayed warm in this place?

CURTIS: I guess they had woven mats and things. Blankets. Some of the ledges and little cubbyholes maybe kept off part of the rain and snow. But it must have been hard, surrounded in here. And nothing much to make fires with.

VALERIE: You think we could make a fire?

CURTIS (*looking around*): I guess it wouldn't hurt. You're supposed to be in a campsite, and it looks like somebody made a fire once, here in these rocks. See if you can find some dead sagebrush or something. (*They leave in opposite directions.*)

A SHAMAN *appears, wearing a gray tunic, his head bound with a white cloth. The* SENTRIES *give him rapt attention. The broken* LEADER, *still kneeling, bends his forehead to the ground like someone badly beaten who refuses to fall. The* SHAMAN *lifts his arms reverently to the sky. One hand holds a medicine stick about four feet long. Feathers, fur, beads, and charms hang from it on a thong. He plants the stick on a rocky ridge, faces the four points of the compass, and leaves.* CURTIS *and* VALERIE *return with some small dry branches.*

VALERIE: Like this?

CURTIS: Yeah, this might do it, with a little dry grass twisted up to start with. *(He lays a fire and nods toward the tote hanging from her shoulder.)* You got any matches in that bag-lady collection of junk?

VALERIE: You know I don't smoke. Don't you have some in the truck?

CURTIS: Bound to. *(He goes to look.* VALERIE *turns slowly, her eyes passing over the* MODOC LEADER *and the medicine stick. She rubs her arms, still cold.)*

VALERIE: Curtis? *(She kneels to break up some twigs.)* It's eerie out here.

CURTIS *(returning)*: Not one stupid match anywhere. My dad doesn't smoke either, and I guess he just——*(He kicks the pile of twigs.)* We're real pioneers, man. *(He hands her a sweater he has brought.)* I found this, though.

VALERIE: I don't need it.

CURTIS: Hey, put it on. You're shivering.

VALERIE *(laying her feather on the table and pulling the sweater over her head)*: You don't have to be nice to me.

CURTIS *(exasperated)*: Was I being nice? Sorry! I keep forgetting myself and doing weird things my parents taught me. It won't happen again, I promise.

VALERIE *(too serious to play along)*: You are nice, Curt. Face it.

CURTIS: And that's what gave you the idea in the first place.

VALERIE: What idea?

CURTIS: The big idea to come on to me like I was suddenly a new invention you couldn't live without.

VALERIE: What are you talking about? You have a really twitchy mind, Curtis. Always cranking corners and throwing people off balance.

CURTIS: You know what I'm talking about. You needed a way to get to Oregon and track down your dad. You didn't have the guts or money to hop a bus and do it yourself. But you didn't mind working *me* over for a couple of weeks till I was ga-ga-gooey enough to steal a truck and head off, any direction you pointed to. You want Oregon? Sure, I'll just go tearing right up the middle of California on this screaming freeway like I know what I'm doing.

VALERIE: You knew what you were doing. Don't try blaming me for that part of it. You wanted to run as bad as I did. You didn't like the way you were living any more than I did.

CURTIS: Nothing was wrong with the way I was living.

VALERIE: That's the whole point, stupid. You've been this nice quiet decent kid with the good grades—forever! You never had a problem because you never made a wave. Curtis—you needed to made a *wave*. A number-nine wave, to see if it was going to drown you or if you could ride it in.

CURTIS: Yeah? *(He sits on the table, as far as he can get from her.)* That's really dumb stuff to think.

VALERIE: No, that dumb stuff is the truth. I did use you, Curt—I admit it. But you used me, too. To test yourself. Am I right? This whole trip has been your test. *(He shrugs and twists the empty paper sack into lumps, unable to meet her eyes. She studies him, her voice going softer.)* Didn't it ever bother you? To *always* do what was expected of you?

CURTIS *(with difficulty)*: Sure. I guess it bothered me. I guess I thought about it, when my folks started planning my life for me, or things like that.

VALERIE: But you didn't do anything about it, Curt.

CURTIS *(giving his life a long slow look, and almost smiling at its ironies)*: Not till now. Not till Miss Valerie Vroom-Vroom put the whammy on me.

VALERIE: Is that a compliment? *(She sits beside him on the table, moved by his pain.)* You know what made me sad when I first noticed you in school? The way you always seemed like you needed to put yourself down. Just because you were serious and kind and curious about things, and—sort of, you know, in love with life. *Besides* being smart and nice. I couldn't understand that, how you could be all those special things and still always seem like you didn't like who you were.

CURTIS: What's so smart and nice about this mess?

VALERIE: Oh, great, Curt. *(The* SENTRIES *stop searching the horizon and lean quietly on their long rifles, curious.)* I know you don't think taking your dad's truck was a really smart idea. Or selling your watch yesterday to get the radiator fixed. But I—I realize you're here in a lava bed with me and the Murdocks because you wanted to help me be happier. That's nice.

CURTIS: Modocs. Not Murdock. Mo-doc.

VALERIE *(softly)*: Okay. Whatever.

> The SENTRIES *smile at each other. The defeated* LEADER *gets to his knees and stares into emptiness, perhaps seeing his people's future.*

CURTIS: I'm sorry the way things turned out for you this morning. Maybe your dad had his reasons for whatever he said, but—man, when you got back to the truck, I thought—the way you looked—

I thought he'd socked you in the mouth or something.

VALERIE: You did? No—he didn't lay a finger on me. Not even a handshake. I was a real shock to him, I guess. He opens the door and there I am, like Hi, I'm Valerie and I've come to live with you, Dad. And his eyes go, Valerie Who?

CURTIS: Yeah. I guess without any warning like that, what could you expect? But when you went in, what happened?

VALERIE: Nothing. He asked how was I. He said he was just about to leave for work. That's what really got to me the most. When he looked at his watch.

> TWO WOMEN *enter and kneel on either side of the* LEADER. *One hands him a morsel of food. He pushes it away, not angrily but so abruptly that it falls from her hand. The* WOMEN *crouch constrained until he finally sighs deeply and holds out his hands to them so they can help him rise. They guide him slowly out of sight.*

CURTIS: But when you explained to him. How things were, and all—

VALERIE: He said it was a bad idea. He asked if my mom had put me up to it. Then he looked at his watch again. Damn—he could've faked it! He could've pretended he was glad to see me, and really wished I could stay with him, but golly gee, he was just starting a three-year job at the South Pole or something and he'd see me when he got back.

CURTIS: He didn't know how to handle it, Val.

VALERIE: He ought to have tried. It would've helped a lot if I could remember he tried. Even *I* take the trouble to lie if it'll make things—not hurt so much! Couldn't he?

CURTIS: Maybe he thought it would be easier on you if he just said right out you couldn't stay with him.

VALERIE: He didn't even *try*.

CURTIS: You scared him, Val. You made him feel—defensive and stuff.

VALERIE: Why do people get that way? Why can't they sit down and say, "Let's talk. Let's listen.

Till we understand each other?" What the blazes
is so hard about that?

CURTIS: I don't know, Val.

> *One of the* SENTRIES *ventures out to find the
> morsel of food, picks the debris off, and shares
> it with his companion. They eat hungrily and
> lick their fingers as they return to their posts.*

VALERIE *(staring into the distance)*: It feels so strange.
All these years my dad's been out there, like some
kind of magic spell I could make. I knew no matter
how bad things got, all I had to say was "Hey, I
don't have to take this. I can go live with him."
And now . . . *(She struggles to keep her voice even.)* All
at once there's not any magic to call on anymore.

CURTIS *(hurting with her)*: Maybe he'll feel different
someday. Maybe even the fact that you came to
him and asked—

VALERIE: It's going to snow, isn't it? The sky's so
heavy. We're going to be found here frozen to a
picnic table, all white and ghosty.

CURTIS *(briskly, relieved that she has regained control)*:
Yeah, it feels really strange to be cold, when you
stop to think that all this rock that we're walking

around on out here was flowing once, red hot, pouring out over trees and grass, and nothing could stop it. *(As he speaks, he goes off left to the truck and returns with a dark bundle.)* And all these little mountains were cinder cones, and the ashes—

VALERIE *(interrupting)*: What's that?

CURTIS: Wrap up in it. You're still shivering.

VALERIE: It's a sleeping bag. *(Shakily, she chooses to laugh instead of cry.)* Oh, man, Curt. Just one sleeping bag? You were thinking ahead, weren't you?

CURTIS *(surprised into defensiveness)*: What's that mean? No. Hey, people take sleeping bags. When they go hunting or something. In case they get stranded or something.

VALERIE: In case they get lucky or something. Were you making big plans for us?

CURTIS: I don't know what you mean. Yeah, I do, but— Okay. It occurred to me. Just wrap up in it. Things turned out different. Okay?

VALERIE *(wrapping herself in it gratefully)*: Thanks. *(She hunts inside it.)* I've lost one of my earrings.

CURTIS: No. You lost it while you were asleep in the truck. *(He pats his shirt pocket.)* I've got it.

VALERIE *(studying his face)*: Oh. *(She wraps herself tightly again.)* I keep thinking about the children, and the old ones. How hard they had it. When it wasn't their fault. Have you read far enough to know what happened?

CURTIS *(referring to the booklet)*: Well, the siege lasted like three or four months, with these sixty guys holding off twelve hundred soldiers. But they were nearly starving, and when they tried to escape to the south over there, they got captured in little groups.

VALERIE: Didn't they ever get their homeland?

CURTIS *(shaking his head)*: The settlers got it.

VALERIE: But it's empty. Couldn't they have *shared* it, even?

CURTIS *(rolling the booklet into a tight cylinder)*: I guess not. And the Army figured hanging the leaders would set the right example. So they did.

VALERIE: Oh, man, that's sad. That's so stupid and sad.

CURTIS: It said when the Army came in here, afterward, they found like this stick that the medicine man had propped up in the rocks. It was supposed to give the Indians victory, you know—stop the bullets and all that. Only it hadn't.

VALERIE: Whatever happened to the other Murdocks?

CURTIS: The Mo— I don't know. It didn't say.

VALERIE (*suddenly bending forward in pain*): Why couldn't he want me, Curt? Why couldn't he be glad I was his kid and wanted to live with him? It stinks. (*She begins to cry.*) It really stinks.

CURTIS: Hey, Val. Don't do that. Listen. Hold out. (*He can't even take her hidden hand.*) You've got to just—hold out. Till it gets better.

VALERIE (*bitterly, still crying*): You figure four months of holding out would do it, Curt? Like the Murdocks?

CURTIS: They tried, Val. Aren't you glad they tried?

VALERIE: But it wasn't enough.

CURTIS: You tried, too, Val. This morning—

VALERIE: But it didn't help.

CURTIS: Listen to me. I was proud of you this morning, walking up to your dad's door. You're
brave—don't ever forget how brave. And you're
way ahead of the Modocs—they had their trou-
bles a hundred years ago, but you're right here—
alive, with everything still ahead for you. *(She
grows quiet as he stumbles on, distressed.)* There's got
to be better things out there, and love, and— I
wish I was the one, because the way I feel about
you—I mean these really deep feelings—but
right now what they're like is—friendship. I don't
know if that means anything to you, but if it
does . . .

VALERIE *(calmly)*: You want me to give up.

CURTIS: No. Just go back. And hold out. That's all.

VALERIE *(testing reality)*: Are your folks going to give
you hell?

CURTIS: I don't know. Usually they act like "Okay,
we see your point." So this is scary, because I
don't know if they'll be that way. Because this
time we're talking really major— *(He turns to her
with a small proud smile.)* A really major wave. *(She*

smiles back faintly, giving him the courage to go on.) You got to remember it's not all your mom's fault either, Val. She's got a right to her own kind of life. I know you think your dad's a real free spirit and all that, but he shouldn't have bailed out on her—he owed you something—

VALERIE *(holding the truth away)*: You know what's funny? All this time I wasn't even thinking about the soldiers. You know? All the soldiers that probably got killed here. Boys from New Jersey or someplace, lying out there on lava rock with bullet holes in them, wondering how their lives turned out so crazy.

CURTIS: Val, if there's maybe times when you need to talk to somebody older than just me, my folks are mostly pretty reasonable. Pretty understanding. Okay?

VALERIE *(trusting him)*: Yeah, Curt. I can tell they must be. It rubbed off on you. *(She stands up and lets the sleeping bag fall.)* I think I want to walk the trail.

CURTIS: You do? Okay. Yeah.

VALERIE: Before it gets too dark.

CURTIS: Okay. Sure. *(He bundles up the sleeping bag*

in such a burst of gratitude that he breaks one of the ties that holds the bag in a roll.)

VALERIE *(hesitating)*: Then maybe ... There's not much point in sitting in the cab of a truck all night in the snow.

CURTIS *(gladly giving her time)*: Well, probably not.

VALERIE *(with difficulty)*: So. We can head back down toward L.A., I guess. It's not like I'm giving up. Or—or settling for just anything. It's just how things are for now. Okay? *(She walks off toward the trail.)*

CURTIS *(almost reaching toward her)*: Okay. It's kind of rough there at first. Go slow. *(She disappears. He stares after her through several moments of silence.)* Val? You okay?

VALERIE *(from offstage)*: Yeah.

CURTIS *(calling, now)*: Don't trip on the rocks— they're sharp. Just take it slow. *(He catches a glimpse of her.)* Hey, you look like a ghost floating along up there.

VALERIE *(from farther away)*: I do? I'm going on around the loop now, Curt. I'll see you.

CURTIS *(calling)*: Yeah. I'll be here.

> *He waits, but there is silence. In it, the drum begins to beat again, a deep heartthrob. He turns his head almost as though he hears it and is seeking its source. He draws a deep breath. With the sleeping bag's broken cord he ties together Valerie's feather, the pop can, and his booklet, and attaches the cord to the stick he used on his hike. He props the stick up on the table with a pile of rocks, and slowly hangs Valerie's earring with the other charms. As he works,* MODOCS *appear, beginning a slow exodus, burdened with bundles. They pass behind him, gray and spent, the young ones helping the old, the spared ones carrying the wounded.*

CURTIS *(softly, in an ordinary voice)*: Just hold out, Val. Okay? Because you can make it. You can. You're going to. I love you, Valerie. But that's for later, when there's not so much to fight.

> *He gathers up the paper sacks and sleeping bag to stow in the truck, and waits, facing the spot where she will reappear. A dwindling line of* INDIANS *continues to pass in the growing darkness. The two* SENTRIES *are the last to go. As*

the drum stops, they glance back at the two medicine sticks standing bravely in the only light that is left.

CURTAIN

NOTE: *Although this play is a fantasy, the Modocs were very real, and their moving story can still be traced in the rocks of the Lava Beds National Monument in the northeast corner of California. Interested readers can write to the Superintendent, Lava Beds National Monument, Box 867, Tulelake, CA 96134. The Visitors' Center there has literature gathered by the Lava Beds Natural History Association, including a booklet called "Captain Jack's Stronghold" (after the Modoc's chief), containing illus-trations from 1873 editions of* Harper's Weekly *and* The Illustrated London News *that would be a great help in planning a production of this play.*

OUIDA SEBESTYEN

It took more than twenty years of frustration before Ouida Sebestyen sold any of the numerous stories, novels, and plays she had written. Once *Words by Heart* was published in 1979, it won a number of accolades, including a Best Book for Young Adults from the American Library Association, one of the year's Ten Best from *Learning Magazine*, and the 1982 American Book Award for best children's fiction in paperback. It was also made into a *Wonderworks* television movie that received two Emmy nominations.

Her success continued with *Far from Home*, *IOU's*, and *On Fire*, the sequel to *Words by Heart*—all stories that celebrate life and strong family relationships.

Sebestyen's theater experiences began in elementary school, where she had all the lead parts, though by junior high school she was a has-been. Nevertheless, she says, "I was reading every play I could get my hands on, and freaking out over movies and operas." After high school she and a friend tried to start a little theater group in their staid West Texas hometown, "with disastrous but hilarious results—a comedy in itself." Later they both wangled jobs backstage at the University of Colorado's Shakespeare Festival, and for several summers they "padded Falstaffs, cloaked kings, and hooked handsome Romeos into their doublets."

Some memories of those times found their way into Ouida Sebestyen's most recent novel, *The Girl in the Box*, an emotional and controversial story about a high school girl who is kidnaped and locked in a dark cellar, where she keeps herself occupied by typing stories, letters, and notes that lead her to self-understanding.

This is Sebestyen's first published play. She lives in Boulder, Colorado.

WORKOUT!

by Sandy Asher

CHARACTERS

RICK, a college freshman, nice-looking, but not in a flashy way. As it is generally easier for a good athlete to fake clumsiness than for a bad athlete to be clumsy on cue, Rick should be played clumsily by a competent dancer.

JACKIE, Rick's classmate, also nice-looking, but not stunning, and a good dancer.

INSTRUCTOR *(offstage voice)*, an aerobic dance teacher.

OTHER STUDENTS *(optional)* If desired, as many members of the aerobic dance class as can fit onstage may participate. They should stand to the sides of and in back of Rick and Jackie. They may react if Rick steps on a toe or bumps one of them but should not compete with the main characters for the audience's attention, particularly during dialogue. There is plenty of time during the dance routines, when nothing is being said, for improvised business related to the situation—the first meeting of a college aerobic dance class.

SETTING

TIME: *The present.*

A college gym. No set or props are needed, but exercise mats or other equipment may be scattered about.

MUSIC: *Ideally, music should be original, perhaps the work of a local or school band, and should be played without vocals. While lively, it should not overwhelm the dialogue. Five pieces, roughly 2–3 minutes each, are needed, in addition to the opening and closing rock theme, which can have lyrics, if desired. The songs may be any combination of rock, country, jazz, marches, etc., and each should maintain a strong, steady beat. The tempo is moderate for the warm-up, increases through the "plateau," and returns to moderate for the cooldown.*

NOTE: *The exercises should make good aerobic sense. "Jazzercise" and "Jane Fonda's Low Impact Aerobic Workout" tapes are good models for music and typical choreography. Three or four movements are repeated in various* combinations for each routine and need not be difficult. RICK does fine on the simpler steps, like marching, but loses it when arm movements, changes of direction, speed, and other small intricacies are added. The point is not to do a slapstick workout but to let a normal workout defeat RICK, as it does most beginners. The dialogue is carried on during the simpler movements, is abandoned as the dancers concentrate on trying something new, is resumed as they get used to a movement, and so on. During the nondialogue moments, INSTRUCTOR may ad lib, occasionally calling out the names of steps, directional changes, words of encouragement. This, too, should not be overdone to the point of drawing attention away from RICK and JACKIE. They, along with the OTHER STUDENTS, if used, should acknowledge INSTRUCTOR's comments with nods, looks of confusion, and appropriate responses, such as straightening their backs, sucking in their stomachs, and so on.

AT CURTAIN RISE: *Rock music is heard and continues through opening business. The curtain opens on a bare stage. If* OTHER

STUDENTS *are used, they enter first, ad libbing everyday conversation, and get seated on floor before* RICK *enters. Or they may already be onstage, seated on the floor, tying their sneakers, talking softly, waiting for class to begin. They ignore* RICK *as he enters, slinking along the back wall, nervously peering about as if searching for people he knows and hoping not to find any. He puts the books he's carrying on the floor near the back wall and, facing the wall, begins to slip off his jeans or sweatpants.*

INSTRUCTOR *(over the music, which begins to fade):* All right, find yourself a place, everybody. Come on. We're running late.

Catching his foot in his jeans as he removes them, RICK *anxiously hops around, finally breaking free. He is now in exercise shorts, a T-shirt, sneakers, and socks. He faces front, takes a deep breath, throws back his shoulders, and—affecting a Tom Cruise strut and perhaps even sunglasses—makes his way to center, nodding to people right and left. He stands there, looking tough, as* JACKIE *enters, hurrying in along back wall. She waves at people, drops her books in a pile next to* RICK'S. *As she pulls off her jeans or sweats, she notices* RICK. *Her face lights up with a broad smile. Music comes to a scratchy halt as a few of the* OTHERS *pull themselves up and take positions to dance.*

INSTRUCTOR: Arm's length, that's all the space you'll need. Let's go, people. On your feet. From now on, I want you in place, dressed out, not later than five after. Got that?

JACKIE hesitates for a moment, psychs herself up, takes a deep breath, then makes her way in and out of the crowd, very purposefully landing herself next to RICK, *perhaps even asking someone else to scoot over, as the next record begins. She smiles at* RICK. *He gives her an ultracool nod. New music begins, of moderate tempo.*

INSTRUCTOR: All right, folks, this is your aerobic warm-up. Working the large muscles first. Lift your feet. Move those arms.

JACKIE, RICK (and OTHERS) begin warm-up. From now on, they keep an eye on INSTRUCTOR, somewhere out above the audience, as if up on a platform, and seem to copy her movements. Occasionally, JACKIE *and* OTHERS *will* change movements and RICK, *involved in other thoughts, will forget to, and then hurry to adjust.* JACKIE *does the routines with ease;* RICK *struggles with both the routine and his nonchalant façade, trying to remain in control whenever she's looking at him, losing it when she turns away, and often in between. As he feels more incompetent, his attitude becomes more "macho."*

JACKIE *(as they dance, to* RICK, *whom she's seen in another class)*: Hi.

RICK *(not recognizing her; using his deepest voice)*: Hi.

INSTRUCTOR: Don't forget to breathe, people. Blow the bad air out. Let the good air in.

RICK *and* JACKIE *breathe as they continue warm-up.*

JACKIE: She's good. *(Nods toward* INSTRUCTOR*)*.

RICK: Oh, yeah? You can tell that, huh? Already?

JACKIE: Oh, sure. She moves well, you can see that right away. But also she tells you to breathe. That's a sure sign of somebody who knows what she's doing. They remind you to breathe.

RICK *(his voice cracking as he temporarily loses his cool façade)*: You mean you could stop breathing from doing this?

JACKIE *(laughing)*: Not really. People sometimes hold their breath, though. The whole point is to take in more oxygen, not less.

> RICK *concentrates hard on breathing as he moves.*

INSTRUCTOR: Warming up those small body parts now. Sending oxygen to the muscles so they'll have plenty to burn. You should be experiencing a slight increase of heart rate.

> RICK *surreptitiously checks his heart and pulse. The movements go to "isolations" of the neck, shoulders, ribs, hips.* RICK *has trouble with this.*

RICK *(in deep voice)*: You know a lot about this stuff, huh?

JACKIE: I thought about becoming an instructor, but, you know, what with starting college and all. I mean, that's enough, don't you think?

RICK: It's plenty. So . . . you're a freshman?

JACKIE: Uh-huh.

RICK: Me too.

JACKIE: Uh-huh.

RICK *(voice rising again)*: You sound like you already knew that.

JACKIE *(She does.)*: Well, I—

RICK *(regaining his façade)*: I mean, it isn't, like, written all over me, is it?

JACKIE *(realizing he doesn't recognize her)*: No, I—

RICK: I didn't think so. So—where are you from?

JACKIE: Philadelphia.

RICK *(voice up)*: No kidding? *(Voice down)* That far?

JACKIE: Yup.

RICK: You're a long way from home.

JACKIE: Guess so.

INSTRUCTOR: Lift up on the rib cage. That's it. Good. Keep your toes pointed forward, knees bent directly over the toes.

RICK *(after arranging his body parts)*: First time away?

INSTRUCTOR: And right and left.

JACKIE: Oh, no. Over the summer, a friend and I backpacked all over Europe.

RICK (*forgetting his cool stance*): No kidding?

INSTRUCTOR: And right and left.

JACKIE: That was my graduation present. The airfare. From my grandparents.

RICK: Nice present.

JACKIE: Yeah. I earned all the spending money, though. Not that we spent much. Youth hostels. Bread and cheese, three times a day. You know how it is.

RICK (*He doesn't, but he's not letting on.*): Oh, sure.

INSTRUCTOR: Down to the hips, now. Right, two. Left, two. Keep those arms moving. And breathe.

JACKIE (*after letting out the bad air*): So, where are you from?

RICK (*using the dance steps as a way to mumble answer away from her*): Right across town.

JACKIE: Beg your pardon?

RICK: Oak Ridge.

JACKIE: Oak Ridge?

RICK: It's a . . . a kind of a suburb. *(She still looks puzzled.)* It's right across town. I live right across town.

INSTRUCTOR: And down to the feet, now. Toes. Toes. Heels. Heels.

JACKIE: Oh. Then you're not in a dorm?

RICK: Sure, I'm in a dorm. What's the point of going to college if you're not in a dorm?

JACKIE: I just thought, you know, since you live right across—

RICK: My parents live right across town. I live in a dorm. Hill Hall.

JACKIE: Oh, great! I'm in Cooper. Right across the drive.

RICK *(too cool to care)*: Great.

> *Music stops. New song begins, somewhat faster, but not frantic. The dance steps reflect this increased tempo with more energy, especially in arm movements.*

INSTRUCTOR: Okay, people, we're heading up the curve now. Heart rate picking up.

JACKIE: How come you chose aerobic dance for P.E.? Most guys won't go near it.

RICK (*grinning*): I know. My brother recommended it.

JACKIE: Your brother goes here too?

INSTRUCTOR: If you get out of breath at any point, I want you to take it a little easier. Got that?

> RICK *and* JACKIE *nod.* RICK *eyes* JACKIE *to see if she's taking it a little easier. She's not. He pushes to keep up.*

RICK: Yeah. He's a senior. Football scholarship. He's a linebacker. Don't ask me to introduce you to him.

JACKIE: I wasn't planning to.

RICK (*beginning to gasp*): Good. He's booked up through 2005.

INSTRUCTOR: You should be able to carry on a conversation without gasping for breath.

> RICK *shoots her a dirty look, works on breathing.*

JACKIE: He's got a girl?

RICK: He's got enough girls to last him through 2005—if he holds it down to one a day.

INSTRUCTOR: Listen to your own body, folks. It'll tell you what to do.

JACKIE: How about you? Are you booked up till 2005?

RICK: Oh, yeah. At least.

JACKIE: Are you on the football team too?

INSTRUCTOR: As long as you keep moving, your fat cells won't know if you're doing the right steps or not. They'll burn.

RICK *(Gives her an incredulous look.)*: You—uh—don't *know* football, do you?

JACKIE: Nope.

RICK: I didn't think so. Well, um, I'm thinking about it. The team. I haven't made up my mind yet—about which position to play.

JACKIE *(Makes sense to her.)*: Oh.

RICK: Anyway, Coach made the guys take this class

a couple years back. To build stamina and coordination.

JACKIE: He's right. It does.

RICK: Maybe. But that's not why my brother recommended it. Ninety-nine girls for every guy is
what he said. Girls in leotards and tights. You
gotta see it to believe it, he said. *(He looks around,
appreciatively, at everyone but* JACKIE.) And here I
am, seeing it and believing it.

JACKIE: Oh.

RICK *(tongue all but hanging out)*: Oh, yeah.

INSTRUCTOR: Heads up. Shoulders back. Suck in
those stomachs. And breathe!

> RICK *pretends to pant at a girl in a notable
> leotard.* JACKIE *rolls her eyes in disgust and
> groans. The music stops. A new song begins,
> this one very lively.*

INSTRUCTOR: We're at the top of the curve now.
You should be working at your target heart rate.
Let those fat cells burn!

> *The routine and pace are too brisk for conver-
> sation. Pretending to ignore* RICK, JACKIE *gets*

into the exercise and performs it well. RICK *picks up on the challenge, but it soon becomes evident that* JACKIE *is outdancing him. He becomes increasingly confused, out of breath, and concerned with his failure to keep up with her. By the end of the song, he's moved himself several paces back and she's grinning trium- phantly. As music ends, she turns and notices where he's gotten to and what bad shape he's in back there. Confident in her victory, she takes pity on her conquest and smiles more kindly.*

INSTRUCTOR *(before next tune begins)*: Keep your feet moving, people. Don't stop cold just because the music stops.

JACKIE *(Jogs in place and waves* RICK *up beside her again. He moves up, barely able to shuffle his feet.)*: Don't give up. You'll catch on. After the first couple of times, you'll be an old hand at it.

INSTRUCTOR *(New music begins. Tempo and movements are now back to moderate.)*: Coming down the back of the curve now. You've survived the worst of it.

RICK *(ticked off that she knows he's done badly)*: Quite

the little expert, aren't you? What is it—you do this all the time? This is your hobby? Your a-vo-ca-tion?

JACKIE: My mom and I went to a class in Philly three times a week—

RICK *(mocking her)*: Your mom? Your *mom*? You and your mom hang out together a lot?

JACKIE: Hey, look, I don't know what your problem is, but leave my mom out of it, okay? If I want to hang out with my mom, I'll hang out with my mom. I mean, it's not as if I'm the one going to college right across town from my folks, is it?

RICK *is stung; his mouth opens and snaps shut.*

INSTRUCTOR: Nice and easy now. You should feel your heartbeat slowing down. *(As* RICK *and* JACKIE *glare at each other)* This is your aerobic cooldown.

RICK *and* JACKIE *finish out this segment in silence, but obviously furious at one another. Music ends. Another song begins, even slower. They begin final stretching movements.*

INSTRUCTOR: Your muscles are nice and warm now. This is the best time to stretch them.

RICK (*softening after a few moments. If he's wearing sunglasses, he removes them now.*): Hey, listen, I shouldn't have said that stuff. I'm sorry.

JACKIE (*softening too*): It's okay. Me too.

RICK: I don't know what came over me. I'm not usually like that. I'm not usually—dancing in a room full of girls in leotards.

JACKIE: What are you usually like?

RICK: Well, I'm not a football player. And I'm not booked up until 2005, either.

JACKIE: I didn't think so.

RICK: It is written all over me, isn't it?

JACKIE: What?

RICK: What I am. What I'm not.

JACKIE: No, it's not. What are you?

INSTRUCTOR: After a solid aerobic workout, your muscles are at their most flexible.

RICK (*completely dropping any Tom Cruise pretensions*): I'm a math major.

INSTRUCTOR: Stretching replenishes the supply of oxygen—and keeps you from stiffening up.

RICK: A freshman and a math major in a room full of girls in leotards. And who notices, right? Who could get excited about a freshman and a math major?

JACKIE: Only another freshman and a math major.

RICK *(ruefully)*: Yeah. Right.

JACKIE *(after a pause)*: I'm a math major.

RICK: You are? You're not! Really?

JACKIE: I saw you this morning in Mr. Kellerman's class.

RICK: Calculus? You're in my Calc I class?

JACKIE: Third row, first seat. You were by the window.

RICK: You noticed that? All the way across the room?

JACKIE *(laughing)*: It was just two rows. But yes, I noticed.

RICK *(flattered; growing reflective)*: I wanted to start all over again in college, you know? I figured, okay, I'm not too far from home—it's all we can afford—but there are 25,000 students here. They can't *all* know what a jerk I was in high school.

JACKIE: I'll bet you weren't a jerk.

RICK: Well, I wasn't . . . everything I wanted to be. I wasn't anything *anybody* wanted to be. So I wanted to start over.

JACKIE: As somebody else? As your brother?

RICK: Pretty dumb, huh?

JACKIE (*shaking her head, "no, not really"*): I wanted to start over, too. As me, but different. I'm pretty shy, usually. You're right, I do hang out with my mom a lot.

RICK: You traveled all over Europe.

JACKIE: That was *places.* I'm good at places. I'm not so good with people. I have one best friend. But now I'm here and she's back in Philly. So I decided, this time around, if I saw something—somebody—I liked, I was going to . . . go for it.

RICK (*nodding, then slowly realizing she means him*): Yeah?

JACKIE (*a bit shyly*): Yeah.

RICK: Say, what's your name?

JACKIE: Jackie.

RICK: I'm Ricky. *(Corrects himself.)* Rick. *(Admits it.)* Ricky.

JACKIE: Hi, Rick.

RICK: Hi, Jackie.

INSTRUCTOR *(as music stops)*: And that's it. A complete aerobic workout. Nice job, people. See you Thursday. And get here on time, okay?

> *The original rock music goes back on, not at full volume.* OTHER STUDENTS, *if any, should exit quickly now, in twos and threes, talking among themselves. One might wave for* JACKIE *to join her, then exit, with a knowing look or a "thumbs up" sign, as she realizes* JACKIE *has other plans.*

RICK *(to* JACKIE*)*: Have you got a class after this?

JACKIE: No, I don't.

RICK: Me neither. Walk you back to the dorm?

JACKIE: Sure. Okay.

RICK *(as they pick up their belongings and head off)*: What do you figure the odds are of two math majors ending up standing next to each other in an aerobic dance class? Astronomical, right?

JACKIE *(smiling triumphantly again)*: Astronomical.

> *They exit, laughing and strutting to the music. Music comes up full.*

CURTAIN

SANDY ASHER

Sandy Asher has been involved with the theater since kindergarten, first performing in plays and dance troupes and then writing her own plays. While in high school in Philadelphia, she performed with the LaSalle College Masque and wrote and performed in the Germantown High School senior class play in 1960. At Indiana University she majored in theater and spent her summers living and performing on a Mississippi River showboat, the last traveling showboat in America.

By the time she published her first novel for young adults, Sandy Asher had written over fifty short stories, dozens of poems, numerous articles, and seven children's plays. Her novels for young adults are usually about ordinary teenagers in difficult situations in school or with their families. For example, a rather quiet eighth-grade girl finds herself embroiled in controversy over an innocent article she writes for the school newspaper in *Summer Smith Begins*. A shy teenager faces anti-Semitism in *Daughters of the Law*. In *Things Are Seldom What They Seem* teenage girls have to deal with the sexual advances of their drama teacher. And a girl has to come to terms with her own and her mother's grief after her father dies in *Missing Pieces*.

Asher has received over a dozen playwriting awards and a National Endowment for the Arts Fellowship Grant for her plays, which range from one-act adaptations of fairy tales to full-length pieces for general audiences. Her most recent play is *A Woman Called Truth*, a one-act celebration of the life of abolitionist and former slave Sojourner Truth, which has been performed in secondary schools in Houston, Texas, and in the New York area, including at The Open Eye: New Stagings in New York City.

She is currently Writer-in-Residence at Drury College in Springfield, Missouri. Her most recent books are *Everything Is Not Enough* and *Wild Words! How to Train Them to Tell Stories.*

CAGES

by Walter Dean Myers

CHARACTERS

ELLEN

JOHN

PEGGY

MARIA

WILLIE

YOSHIRO

OLIVER

SETTING

A bare and darkened stage. There are background crowd noises such as those heard at a sports event. The noise subsides gradually until it is barely audible. A full thirty seconds pass before two players rise from the audience and go to the stage. They produce chalk and draw squares on the floor of the stage. They settle into the squares, quite comfortably. A few seconds later the other players follow them onto the stage and draw their own squares. All the squares are lit by spots.

Throughout the play the actors read newspapers and occasionally leave their cages to drink from a water fountain at the back of the stage. It is clear that the interiors of the cages are warm while outside the cages it is cold.

There is a chair toward back of stage, barely visible.

YOSHIRO: I've got a plan.

WILLIE: Yeah, you always got a plan. That's why we still here. Following your plans.

ELLEN: Why don't you shut up? At least he's trying.

WILLIE: Look, I'm the only one that can get us out of this mess. I've got the power, the strength. And . . . I've got the will to use my strength. I'm from a race of warriors, man. . . .

ELLEN: Has anybody heard about the fighting? I mean, if they're coming by way of the river, they should be here soon.

WILLIE: My people will be here before your people. Then we'll see what the real deal is.

ELLEN (*getting out of the cage, as does* WILLIE): Do you really believe that your fighters have a chance? I wouldn't mind . . .

YOSHIRO: You can't just switch sides like that. You have to decide what you want to do. You have to believe in something.

ELLEN: I believe . . . I believe in survival! I know we're not getting out of this alive. I just know it! Grief, it's freezing out here. (*Reenters cage.*)

WILLIE: Talk for yourself, Mama. I'm definitely making it, because I Am The Kid!

PEGGY: Anybody know a four-letter word for surrender?

JOHN: How about cede? C-e-d-e.

PEGGY: Good, it fits.

MARIA: What was your plan, Yosh?

YOSHIRO: I think we should keep as quiet as possible. They don't know we're here, right? If we keep quiet, they'll probably pass right by us.

WILLIE: Later for that lame noise. I say we attack! We jump up and take them on. Otherwise they won't show us no respect.

JOHN: How can we fight them from these cages? I can't reach out more than a foot. *(Reaches out and swings.)*

WILLIE: I say we hold our ground. . . .

PEGGY *(Looks up from reading.)*: In the cages?

WILLIE: In the cages! Then when the suckers get close, we strike for the heart!

MARIA: It might work.

YOSHIRO: But it'll be risky! I still say we'll be better off if we keep quiet. Maybe they're headed west.

ELLEN: We can compromise. Some of us can attack and some of us can just be quiet.

YOSHIRO: No—if anybody attacks, they'll look for the rest of us.

ELLEN *(Steps out of cage, smoothes skirt.)*: Maybe they'll like us. Maybe they'll think we're . . . you know, attractive.

PEGGY: I haven't had a lot to say so far, but I don't think being attractive is the way to go. I was looking at my crystal before, and I got these really strange vibes. *(Continues talking despite the fact that nobody is listening to her.)*

MARIA: Has anybody talked to them? Are you sure that they want to harm us?

WILLIE: Are you crazy, woman? Do you think they're coming here because they've got nothing else to do? They think we're garbage. They don't even want us in their world because they think they're better than we are.

YOSHIRO: What . . . what do you think they'll do?

PEGGY: Okay, first they're probably going to try to take our souls. I mean if they get our souls, then they can control our past karma. It's not so important that they control our future karma, but if they get our past karma, then it's, like, all over.

YOSHIRO: They'll rape the girls.

ELLEN *(seductively)*: If that's what they have in mind, maybe we can work something out.

JOHN: Quiet. I hear noises!

> *There is quiet on the stage as all the players crouch low in their cages. The sounds of the baseball game rise. The announcer describes a long home run. Finally the noises subside.*

PEGGY: That was close.

MARIA: Too close.

YOSHIRO: We're doomed. We'll never defeat them.

JOHN: Doomed? That's an archaic word. People don't say doomed.

YOSHIRO: What do they say?

JOHN: Wasted. Jacked up. Anything you want, but not doomed.

ELLEN *(with growing desperation)*: Who cares if we're doomed or wasted? I mean really, who cares? Willie, you said you could do something! Now, can you do it or are you just a . . . a . . .

WILLIE: A what? A what? *(Furious, rushes out of cage.)*

ELLEN: A punk! A nothing! A turkey! A boy! A boy!

WILLIE: Don't you call me no boy!

> *They begin to tussle. The tussle becomes more and more sensual.*

JOHN: Hey, why don't you two knock it off? Why don't you . . . Hey, get off of her! If I wasn't in this cage, I'd break your head, Willie. *(Tries to get out of cage but can't.)*

> WILLIE *and* ELLEN, *wrestling on the floor, have suddenly become aware of the proximity of their bodies.* PEGGY *is covering her face but peeking through her fingers.*

ELLEN *(breaking away from* WILLIE*)*: Okay, okay, enough! I'm sorry. I'm sorry.

WILLIE: Well, you'd just better be. You'd just better be sorry.

ELLEN: You're hurting my wrist. *(He lets go.)* God, you're strong. What are you, anyway? A weight lifter or something?

WILLIE: A man's supposed to be strong.

JOHN: Look, there's another way.

MARIA: Good. What is it?

YOSHIRO: Listen! What was that noise?

They all listen to the silence.

JOHN: It's nothing. We're all just jumpy. Look, it's clear we're not all going to make it. What we have to do is to decide which of us is going to make it and which of us isn't. We know that we look like them. So when they come here, we decide which of us is going to make it. Then we ... you know ... the others. ...

MARIA: What ... what do you mean, "you know"?

JOHN: We have to sacrifice the others.

MARIA: Sacrifice? *(Realizing what he means)* Oh, God! *(She begins to weep softly.)*

YOSHIRO: I see what he means. When they see us ... sacrificing ... those who have to be sacrificed, maybe they'll think we're with them.

ELLEN: You wouldn't sacrifice any of the women, would you?

JOHN: Everybody's the same! Everybody's the same! We draw straws! I've got some straws we can use.

PEGGY: It could work. We could pick the ... is sacrificee a word?

MARIA: Victim. The word you're looking for is victim.

PEGGY: Well, all right. At any rate, we could pick the victim by tarot cards.

JOHN: We could just pick the black guy.

WILLIE: Racist son of a ...

JOHN: It doesn't have anything to do with race, man. You just happen to be the only black guy here, that's all. It's like a natural selection. It's not like it's personal.

WILLIE: I'm going to get me a victim right now!

(Struggles against the bars of his cage. His face contorts with the rage, and with the effort. He is unable to free himself.)

YOSHIRO: Willie, why can't you be reasonable? You're the only one here brave enough to die. You're a warrior. Your death won't be like ours. Next to you we're nothing.

WILLIE: What?

PEGGY: In your past life you were probably a king or something. Have you ever channeled back in time? You really should, because then you would really know how great you were.

WILLIE: I ain't being no victim.

MARIA: You *have* had experience.

WILLIE: I'm not being a victim!

ELLEN: We'll give you a warrior's sendoff. Maybe sacrifice a virgin or something. Peggy, are you . . . you know . . .

PEGGY: Not exactly.

ELLEN: Maria?

MARIA: This is really crazy. We're acting as if we're

some primitive people back in the Stone Age. How can we talk about sacrificing people?

WILLIE: I will not be a victim.

YOSHIRO *(in despair)*: Nothing's going to work. We're all going to be killed. Killed! I can't stand it! I can't stand it! *(He rushes out of his cage and runs offstage.)*

They all get out and look at YOSHIRO, *who's offstage.*

ELLEN: Oh, no! He's running right toward the river.

MARIA: But he's running!

PEGGY: It could be an anxiety attack. I had an aunt once who had anxiety attacks, and everyone thought she was, like, really weird. Then she started acupuncture and it didn't help her attacks but it really helped her complexion. With Yoshiro I think it's definitely anxiety.

MARIA *(joyfully)*: But he's running away! He's doing something!

JOHN: For now. He won't last two minutes out there.

ELLEN: If we knew he was going to be like that, he could have been the victim.

JOHN: Well, he's gone. I never did trust his type anyway. He was too uptight, if you ask me.

They all return to their cages.

PEGGY: We have to get on with the business of what we are about.

WILLIE: About being free. That's what it's all about. If I was free, I could make my moves.

MARIA: I think Willie is right. We do need to be free.

PEGGY: I have a plan.

WILLIE: You also have your foot out your cage.

PEGGY *(bringing her foot back into the cage)*: I've been looking at the locks on these cages. And I've come to the conclusion that I can make a key to open them. I used to make copper earrings, and I just know I could make a key.

WILLIE: How you gonna make a key? Huh? You a locksmith? If you're not a locksmith, it's illegal to make a key.

MARIA: But if she could make a key—

JOHN: Listen, who cares if she can make a key? Who cares? Huh? *(Gets out of cage and comes center stage.)* If she's not a locksmith who has a legal license, then her making a key becomes illegal, right? Freedom without law isn't worth a red nickel. If I break the law, I don't deserve to be free.

ELLEN: You've got to be kidding. We stay in these cages and we're going to be killed. I don't want to die. I don't know how plainly I can say that. I don't want to die.

JOHN: Somebody's coming!

MARIA: I'm so afraid.

WILLIE: Everybody quiet.

> *There is the sound of running footsteps, and then* OLIVER *enters. He looks from side to side, obviously distressed. He recoils from the people in the cages, then relaxes.*

PEGGY: Who . . . who are you?

OLIVER *(panting)*: I'm called Oliver. I'm from the high country, and I've been running for days. Who are you people?

PEGGY: We're refugees too. We're trapped in these cages. Unless we can find a way to get out, we're probably doomed. *(Looks at John.)* Maybe wasted.

MARIA: How are things out there? Is it safe?

OLIVER: Safe? What a joke. It's brutal out there. I just barely made it here.

JOHN: Look, man, we're friendly. You can rest here.

OLIVER: Thanks, I appreciate it.

> *He looks around, pulls chalk from his pocket, and then makes his own cage over Willie's. He brings a chair from the rear of the stage and sits on the back of it so he is higher than* WILLIE.

WILLIE: We can still get out of this mess if— *(Notices* OLIVER *on chair.)* Hey, what the heck are you doing in my cage?

OLIVER: What makes this your cage? You have your name on it? Where's your name?

WILLIE: I was here first, man.

OLIVER: I got nothing against you being here. We can share a cage. That's, like, brotherhood.

WILLIE: Yeah . . . well, maybe. But I don't want you sitting there over me.

JOHN: Give the guy the top cage, for Pete's sake. What does it mean to you?

ELLEN: I really didn't see your name on the cage, Willie.

WILLIE: He's gonna see my name upside his head if he don't get away from here.

> *They tussle, rolling around on the floor. The players run out, separate the two fighters, and then hurry back to their cages. WILLIE scrambles back to his cage. OLIVER sulks, shivering, at stage left.*

MARIA: If we don't cooperate, we'll be here forever.

PEGGY *(working on making a key)*: She's right. If we don't get some plan going, we might as well give up.

ELLEN: I think it's too late already. We may never be free.

JOHN: That's because your very concept of freedom is wrong, baby. Freedom is what you make of it. It's a feeling, a sensation. It's a warm breeze off the ocean. I think . . . I think . . . I think I'm free already.

PEGGY: Oh, splendid. Drop us a postcard.

WILLIE: You're in a cage just like the rest of us. You're not free. What do you want and go lie about it for?

JOHN: I'm free already. They got my body locked up in this cage, but my mind's wandering around the Milky Way, light-stepping through a purple sunset.

OLIVER: What are you, a liberal?

WILLIE: Ain't nothing wrong with liberals.

JOHN: Woo! My soul's tripping on Mars right now.

PEGGY: In all fairness, John, you're not helping us very much. I don't mean that you're not free or anything, but—

ELLEN: Your foot's out again.

PEGGY: Sorry. *(She brings her foot back in.)* These cages are getting cramped. Anyway, we have to at least agree what freedom is.

OLIVER *(still sulking, still shivering out of his cage)*: It's a feeling. A sensation of lightness. A vision.

JOHN: I know what you mean. A vision! I see it! Venus is opening her arms to me! I see angels dancing along the rings of Saturn. I see myself dancing and laughing along the crease of the universe! *(He is dancing about the stage.)*

MARIA: Maybe we should pool our resources. Let's find out what each of us can do. Maybe we'll come up with something.

PEGGY: Well, I mentioned that I think I can make a key. I used to make copper jewelry down in the Village. I used to sell it on St. Mark's Place.

MARIA *(wistfully)*: Villages, towns, they all seem so far away.

JOHN: I hope you're not going to start boohooing.

PEGGY: Let's each give his or her background. I'll start *(Recites formally.)* I attended Urbanvale Parochial School, where I excelled in the majority of the liberal arts subjects. Then I went to Switzerland for two years, studying under private tutors, and then to Vienna, where I completed my education in the classics. Upon returning to the United States of America, I made my social debut at the University Club and was then engaged to

Mr. William R. Callahan the Third, son of William R. Callahan the Second, prominent businessman and patron of the arts.

ELLEN: This is ridiculous. We're trapped here and she's making pretty speeches. Let's start a fire. Maybe someone will notice it and rescue us.

OLIVER: We don't have anything that'll burn.

ELLEN: We can burn our clothes.

JOHN: Keep your clothes on. Go on, Peggy.

WILLIE: Yo, man, let that girl burn her clothes if she wants.

JOHN (*to* ELLEN): Go ahead, Ellen, it's your turn.

ELLEN: I'm not going through that nonsense. Anyway, my background is my business.

JOHN: Look, I'll go. I mean I don't have anything complex—I'm a simple guy.

OLIVER: He just wants sympathy. Don't give it to him.

JOHN: All I want, all I've ever wanted, was just somebody to care for me. Is that so much? Is that really so much to ask? That a fellow human being care? Is it really that much?

There is a long pause. JOHN *is still distraught.*

OLIVER *(quietly)*: I care for you, John.

JOHN: What?

OLIVER *(with effort)*: I care for you, John.

JOHN: What are you, queer or something? I noticed you got real soft-looking hands. You queer?

OLIVER: Hey, you're a real creep! You know that? You're a real creep!

JOHN: See, he hates me! He hates me. Even the damned queers hate me. What's this country coming to when even the queers go around hating you?

MARIA: Please, oh please. We've got to do more than this. We've got to find a way to free ourselves and be who we are, or who we were, or . . . or something!

PEGGY: Okay, I have a little trouble with that. I mean, it's like I have a very shaky holistic condition when we're speaking karma-wise. I was once channeling; it was a very heavy trip and I was going through a Tibetan monk back to a time that just might have been, like, prehistory. And just when I was reaching a really ultimate experience, I was cross-channeled by something that had to be truly evil. . . . *(She continues as others talk.)* And what I think really happened was that I was having an Egyptian-Mayan cross-experience, which has a completely different channeling concept because their calendar was based on the star Betelgeuse before the splinter group broke off from the Nile area and crossed over to North America, and . . .

MARIA *(ignoring* PEGGY, *who continues talking)*: I think I'm losing my sense of what's real and what's not real. Is this all real?

OLIVER *(dramatically)*: It was real enough out there. It was real enough when you saw the light of flares on the men's faces, the fear in their eyes. *(He wanders toward* WILLIE's *cage.)* It was real enough when you realized how cheap life was on the front lines. *(*OLIVER *sits on chair in* WILLIE's *cage as he continues.)* It was real enough when you heard the cries and saw the blood and the body bags.

Oh, God, please don't let me think about the body bags.

WILLIE *(noticing that* OLIVER *is over him again)*: Hey, what you doing?

> WILLIE *and* OLIVER *fight viciously.*

PEGGY: Stop them!

MARIA: Please!

JOHN *(running between* WILLIE *and* OLIVER*)*: Come on, guys! Hey, we can work this out. Look, Willie, why don't you take the cage Yoshiro had?

WILLIE: Yeah, okay.

> *He's breathing hard and giving* OLIVER *dirty looks. He goes over and establishes himself in* YOSHIRO's *cage. Whereupon* OLIVER *immediately moves the chair to the new cage.* WILLIE *and* OLIVER *start to fight again, and all the players come out of their cages to break them up.*

OLIVER: God, these people cause trouble. *(He goes back to Willie's original cage, obviously disgruntled.)*

JOHN: I hear noises!

The players are huddling in their cages, trembling, except for MARIA. *The sound of the baseball game is louder, perhaps nearer. There is the unmistakable sound of a child's laughter. Finally, the noises diminish. The players begin to stir again.*

ELLEN: I don't know how much longer I can take these close calls.

MARIA: Laughter. I'm sure I heard laughter. It sounded like a child.

WILLIE: I'm getting an ulcer.

OLIVER: It's just gas. You people don't get ulcers.

WILLIE: Why don't you die, turkey?

PEGGY: I think I have it! I do! I think I have it!

OLIVER: And us fresh out of antibiotics.

ELLEN: How on earth did you catch anything in that cage? I mean, I know people fool around anywhere, but . . .

PEGGY: No, I mean I think the key I've made works! *(She fiddles with the lock on her cage, then triumphantly flings the cage open.)* There!

WILLIE: She's done it!

JOHN: She's not out yet.

PEGGY *gets out of cage, starts running around.*

OLIVER: That key isn't legal. What you've done is to make an illegal key. We're nothing more than criminals if we use that key.

PEGGY: Oh, don't be ridiculous. Who's going to know? *(She starts going from cage to cage to release the players.)*

OLIVER: Don't come near me! Don't come near me! I don't care what I've done in the past, or how bad it gets, I'm still a moral person! I'm not a criminal!

PEGGY: Willie?

WILLIE: I can't get out of here fast enough. Just turn me loose. That's all I ask. Just turn me loose.

(PEGGY starts to release him.)

WILLIE: Wait. What . . . what are your terms? *(WILLIE, halfway out of cage, stops, looks around, and then retreats back into cage.)*

PEGGY: Terms? What do you mean? I don't have any terms.

WILLIE: Yeah? Look, I ain't going for that bull. Everybody got their terms, man. I ain't going nowhere until I find out what's happening.

OLIVER: What did she say? She won't tell you what the terms are?

WILLIE: She said she didn't have any terms.

MARIA: I think she means it.

OLIVER: The first term she has is that she's made you a criminal.

WILLIE: An escapee!

OLIVER: A runaway!

WILLIE: A fugitive.

OLIVER: Then when she hits you with her other terms, you'll have to take them. That's her little game.

WILLIE: She must think I'm stupid. *(Slaps hands with* OLIVER.*)*

PEGGY: I could come up with some terms. I don't mean anything, like, heavy or anything like that. Just something light. Like maybe you could spend one day a year thinking about me or something.

OLIVER: Here it comes. Now we got Peggy Day.

PEGGY: What's one little day? I mean one little day?

WILLIE: What's wrong with it? It encroaches on my freedom, that's what's wrong with it. Hey, I'm hip to your game, woman.

PEGGY (*going to* JOHN's *cage*): John?

JOHN (*mumbling*): We're safe here.

PEGGY: What?

JOHN (*mumbling again*): We're safe here.

PEGGY (*shouting*): WHAT!

JOHN: We're safe here. We don't know what's out there. I mean, we don't really know, now do we? We don't know what they'd do to us if they found us out of the cages. We don't know anything. And ... and there's that thing that they were saying ... you know, about being criminals ... And there's your terms. I mean, like where do you get off wanting a day and everything? Just where do you get off?

MARIA: Peggy?

PEGGY: Okay, I'll drop the Peggy Day. You want to use the key or not?

JOHN *(curling up)*: I'm safe here. You can't give me that. When you guarantee that I'll be safe, then I'll leave. *(Uncurls.)* It's a matter of survival. What good is . . . anything if you don't survive? I mean . . . *(Trails off to mumbling.)*

MARIA: Peggy?

PEGGY: Ellen?

ELLEN: I would go, but I won't go without Willie.

PEGGY: Willie?

OLIVER: What the heck do you want with that guy?

ELLEN: He wants me. He thinks I'm, you know—

WILLIE: Sexy, beautiful . . .

OLIVER: It's no wonder they keep you people in cages.

JOHN: Willie, look, you're always running your mouth about freedom, man. If you want freedom, you're going to have to start acting like a decent human being.

WILLIE: Man, go to—

ELLEN: I don't feel the way they do, Willie. I'll wait

for you. We'll either be free together *(heroically)* or we'll . . . we'll . . .

JOHN: You'll what?

ELLEN: I don't know. But whatever it is . . . hand in hand, we'll do it together!

WILLIE: You and me. Together. Now and forever!

ELLEN: Maybe not right now. I mean, we're kind of locked up and everything, you know.

MARIA: Peggy?

PEGGY: Maria?

MARIA: Can you unlock my cage?

PEGGY: Sure.

> *She goes over and unlocks* MARIA's *cage.* MARIA *slowly, cautiously, leaves cage.*

OLIVER: You'd better get back in there before you get blown away, girl.

MARIA: No. I don't . . . I don't want to. I want to go away from here.

JOHN: She's afraid of what's going to happen to her.

If Willie gets loose. I mean he's already said he's going to mess with Ellen.

PEGGY (*Runs over and locks Willie's cage.*): There!

WILLIE: What did you do that for? I got to be free. I *got* to be free!

MARIA: I want to take a chance. I'm a little afraid, but . . .

ELLEN: Lock me in! If one of my fellow creatures is not free, then none of us is free! I can't be free if Willie is not free.

PEGGY (*locking* ELLEN's *cage*): Okay.

MARIA (*taking tentative steps across stage*): I have to take a chance. Something inside, I don't even know what it is, says that I'm not alive here. I'm not alive unless I go out there.

JOHN: You'll never survive.

MARIA: Oh, please, somebody come with me. Somebody take a chance with me.

OLIVER: You're out of your mind. You go out there and you're dead meat.

MARIA: Peggy. You made the key. Come with me.

It can't be worse than this. I heard laughter. Did you hear the laughter? People are actually laughing somewhere. If they can laugh . . .

JOHN: They can kill. Man is the only animal that laughs and kills.

WILLIE: That kills the flesh and the spirit.

OLIVER: We have a way to be, a place to be. These cages aren't perfect, but at least here we're not criminals. We're not running around out there not knowing what's going to happen from day to day. I reject the life of the criminal!

MARIA: We could be good criminals. Criminals who laugh and run and whatever it is that criminals do. Oh, Peggy, won't you come with me?

PEGGY: I really want to go with you. I want to go so badly I can taste it. I really do. But you can't go out there and *resist*. That's what they're doing out there. That's what's *making* the conflict. Can't you see that? You have to give in, to surrender to the forces that are trying to defeat you. It's like Tai Chi Chuan: You allow the forces to come into you and through you until there's nothing left to resist. That way all force is nullified, all power is reduced to nothingness. The force and power of war are reduced to the submissiveness and gentility of peace. Can you see what I'm saying?

MARIA: No, I don't see. I don't see and I'm afraid and I don't know what's out there. But I have to go. I have to go and try to be part of it.

PEGGY (*Gets back in cage, folds hands in front of her*): Ooooommmmmmmmmmmmmmmmmmm . . .

MARIA: Oh. (*Takes a deep breath and runs offstage.*)

JOHN: She's a fool!

ELLEN: I can't believe her. I mean, she looks so cool and everything.

OLIVER: Listen!

> *The noises rise, and the players huddle in fear. There is a very loud sound of the baseball game. Some of the players tremble. Finally, the noises subside.*

> *One by one the players, badly shaken, get up. Then there is the sound of footsteps. The players again huddle and shake as the footsteps draw near. From offstage* YOSHIRO *runs wildly onto*

*the stage, looks around, and dives into the cage
vacated by* MARIA. *He keeps his hands over his
head for a while, then finally looks up, as do
the other players.*

JOHN: Yosh?

YOSHIRO: Who's there?

JOHN: It's me, John.

YOSHIRO: Thank God I made it back. *(They all come
out of their cages to embrace* YOSHIRO.*)*

WILLIE: What's it like out there, man?

YOSHIRO: Terrible, terrible.

ELLEN: Were you hurt?

YOSHIRO: No, I got past them.

JOHN: Maria's gone.

YOSHIRO: I know.

ELLEN: You know?

YOSHIRO: She's with the others. On the way here
I was hiding in the underbrush when I saw them
coming by. At first I had my head down, but then
I looked up, and there she was.

OLIVER: How—how did she look?

YOSHIRO: I couldn't tell. She had her face turned away from me, headed toward the river.

ELLEN: The river? Oh, no.

JOHN: Hey, that's the way it goes. We'll just have to forget about her.

WILLIE: Let's have a moment of silence for her. It's the least we can do.

They are all silent. The lights dim. From the distance comes the muffled sound of a baseball game.

CURTAIN

WALTER DEAN MYERS

Born in West Virginia and raised in Harlem, Walter Dean Myers lives in Jersey City, New Jersey, and is the author of a number of prize-winning novels for young adults. Among his earliest books are *Fast Sam, Cool Clyde, and Stuff*; *It Ain't All for Nothin'*; and *The Young Landlords*, all named Notable Books for Young Adults by the American Library Association. *The Young Landlords* also received the Coretta Scott King Award and was made into a film. Myers's *The Legend of Tarik*, the story of a young black knight, was named a Best Book for Young Adults by the ALA. He has also won praise for his two novels about corruption in high school and college basketball, *Hoops* and *The Outside Shot*. His recent novel about a Harlem gang, called *Scorpions*, was named a Newbery Honor Book.

Myers has also written books for children—including *The Dragon Takes a Wife*, *The Golden Serpent*, *Mr. Monkey and the Gotcha Bird*, *Adventure in Granada*, and *The Hidden Shrine*.

Among his other publications for young adults are two mystery-adventures: *Tales of a Dead King*, set in Egypt, and *The Nicholas Factor*, set in the jungles of the Amazon; *Motown and Didi: A Love Story*, a realistic account of the struggles of inner-city life; *Sweet Illusions*, an unusual look at teenage pregnancy in which readers are invited to write endings to each chapter; *Crystal*, the inside story of an attractive girl's efforts to make it to the top of the New York fashion world; and his highly acclaimed Vietnam War novel *Fallen Angels*, which also received the Coretta Scott King Award. His most recent novels are *Me, Mop, and the Moondance Kid* and *The Mouse Rap*.

Walter Dean Myers is currently working on a play about Paul Robeson.

WAR OF
THE WORDS

by Robin F. Brancato

CHARACTERS

THE NOTES:

HOMER, the leader

DANTE

WILLIAM

GUINEVERE

DESIREE

LUCINDA, not officially a Note; a new
girl in town, admired by Homer

THE GRUNTS:

BUZZ, the leader

SPIKE

PUNCH

BETTE

DOT

MOLL

War of the Words illustrates the conflict between two rival teenage gangs, The Notes and The Grunts. These adversaries have long struggled to defend their turf—that is, their respective sides of the urban schoolyard. The cause of the contention between them is not ethnic diversity or class rivalries but irreconcilable differences in communication. The Notes are pretentious, effete sissies who speak in iambic pentameter—usually even in rhymed couplets; The Grunts, at the other extreme, speak in clichés, fragments of esoteric slang, and monosyllabic grunts.

The Notes males wear stereotypical outfits that suggest "poet" or "romantic." That is, one wears a velvet jacket, another a cape and beret, the third a shirt with a ruffle at the neck. On the back of each costume is each one's name and an emblem that says "Notes" along with musical notes (♩ ♪), such as would be seen on jackets worn by a typical gang. Their hair is long, and their manners are exaggeratedly polite, even affected.

The Notes females are dressed in frilly clothes, such as *Gone With the Wind*-style hoopskirts, or long dresses of flimsy material, or very feminine peasant dresses. Guinevere and Desiree wear their names and the Notes emblem on their dresses. Their hair is carefully arranged. Lucinda is dressed like the female Notes but with no emblems on her clothing.

The Grunts males, all with crewcuts, are wearing as little clothing as possible because they want their muscles to show. They wear tight jeans or shorts, sleeveless shirts made of fishnet, or skintight T-shirts with slogans such as "The Grunts—Ugh" or "If You Want Me, Grunt."

The Grunts females are decked out in short skirts and low-cut tops in Day-Glo colors. Their hair is teased into bushy halos. They may be wearing Grunt emblems on their outfits also.

War of the Words is intended to include actor and audience participation. The actors are invited, before going into production, to change the script—that is, to add or fuse characters, depending on the number of participants available. Lines consistent with the speech of the two gangs and with the spirit of the play may be added to the existing script, and the poems that make up the competition at the end of the play are to be written, in advance, by the actors.

Music may also be added in appropriate places. For instance, at the outset of the play one of the Notes may be serenading his lady love on a flute or a recorder. The Grunts, especially the females when they are bopping, may also improvise music or rhythm by beating on garbage can lids or other "found" musical instruments. Music may be used throughout as a background and as a part of the competition at the end of the play.

SETTING

A school yard. The stage is divided in half by a length of fence that suggests an insurmountable barrier between the turf of the two gangs, THE NOTES *and* THE GRUNTS. *A painted backdrop shows the exterior of an urban school, complete with basketball hoops, graffiti, and an urban skyline in the distance. Stage right,* THE NOTES' *turf, features a flower-bedecked arbor and three park benches, or fancy garden chairs, or swings. Potted plants, either real or artificial, enhance the* NOTES' *territory. Graffiti on their side include hearts-and-flowers motifs and such sayings as " 'Poetry is the spontaneous overflow of powerful feelings'—Wordsworth."*

The GRUNTS' *turf is makeshift-urban-playground, strewn with such items as old tires, cement pipe, and garbage containers. Graffiti include crude sketches of knives dripping blood*

*and such sayings as "Buzz Don't Take Nothin'
from Nobody" and "Yur Mudder's Got a Mustache."*

*When the curtain opens, the three NOTES
couples are frozen in a romantic tableau.
DANTE is serenading GUINEVERE with a flute.
WILLIAM, kneeling, offers an armful of flowers
to DESIREE, and HOMER, in the center of
NOTES turf, kisses LUCINDA's hand, stares at
her soulfully, and whispers intimate secrets.
Meanwhile the three GRUNTS males are sparring with each other, competing for space at
the peephole in the fence that divides the territories, while THE GRUNTS females slouch near
them, noisily cracking gum and bopping to the
rhythm of a real or imaginary beat.*

SPIKE: Outta my way, punk!

PUNCH: Punch. *Punch* is m'name.

SPIKE: I know your punkin' name as well as I know
my own. *(Tries to remember his own.)* Umm,
umm . . . Spike! That's it, Spike! *(Shoves* PUNCH
with an elbow.) Ain't we been Grunts together since
we was grade school dropouts? Move oveh!

BUZZ *(bending his buddies' arms behind their backs)*:   Hey, Spike, Punch, let *me* look.

SPIKE and PUNCH *(intimidated)*:   Yeah, Buzz, yeah.

BUZZ: *Who's* the boss?

SPIKE and PUNCH: *You* are, Buzz. *You're* the boss.

BUZZ: Don't you forget it. Now, gimme some space. *(Stares through the peephole.)* What the punk are they doing today? Same punkin' sissy stuff like always, talking in poetry?

SPIKE: Yeah, worse than ever! They're gettin' out of hand.

PUNCH: They're pollutin' the air with that poetry, man.

BETTE: And hurting our eyeballs with those gaggy clothes they're wearing!

DOT: Somebody comes by here is gonna think *we're* part of them. Oooo! Noooo!

MOLL *(listening, hand cupped to ear)*:   They call that music? I could make better sounds blowin' into a bottle!

PUNCH: Let's rough up The Notes. Let's rip up their flowers and make holes in that flute.

BETTE: It's already got holes in it.

PUNCH: So *that's* why it sounds so bad.

SPIKE: Let's pound 'em in their voice boxes!

BUZZ: Yeah, they been asking for trouble. They been starting up like this every day.

SPIKE: Makin' low remarks about us. Actin' like they're better than us. Let's—

BUZZ *(shoving* SPIKE *away from the peephole again)*: Shut up and let me hear what they're saying about us.

> SPIKE *and* PUNCH *press their ears to the wall, and* BUZZ *returns to the peephole. The three of them react exaggeratedly to everything they hear with grimaces and gagging sounds.* THE GRUNTS *girls, meanwhile, pay attention off and on, but during the "off" times, they pull out supplies and begin primping and fixing each other's hair. Meanwhile, in* NOTES *territory . . .*

HOMER: Lucinda is your name? When did you come? And tell me all about the place you're from!

LUCINDA *(self-consciously)*: I've . . . I've been here, Homer, for so little time.

> Does everyone who lives here talk in
> rhyme?

DANTE: Not everyone, Lucinda—the elite!
The brains like us, the ones you want to
meet.
Meet Desiree, and William, over here.
I'm Dante, and my love is Guinevere.

WILLIAM: Just don't go over *there*. You'll see The
Grunts!
I'll guarantee you, every one's a dunce.

LUCINDA: I don't quite understand this. Why the
wall?

GUINEVERE: To keep ourselves as pure as possible.

LUCINDA: What do they do to you? How do they
speak?

DESIREE: Like hoodlums. Every one of them's a
freak!

LUCINDA: But aren't they part of this—I mean the
school?

HOMER: They're dropouts, mostly, trying to be cool.
They come here, after school, to taunt and
mock,

And try to run us off the yard and block.

DANTE: It's shameful how they curse, and mangle words,
And call us fairies, sissies, wimps, and nerds!

DESIREE: The things they say! Especially Buzz, the cad!
They've made the neighborhood go down. It's sad!

LUCINDA: And you don't bother them—you're innocent?

HOMER: They *say* we do, because their minds are bent.
They say our voices interrupt their grunts,
And that our music's terrible. And once
They hurled a stink bomb at us, if you please,
Because they said our flowers made them sneeze!

LUCINDA: I know I'm new here, but I can't quite see
Why everyone must talk in poetry. . . .

There is a gradual change, beginning here, in BUZZ's *reactions. He watches* LUCINDA *more attentively through the peephole and begins to listen to her with real interest.* SPIKE *and* PUNCH *continue to overreact to* THE NOTES, *and* BETTE, DOT, *and* MOLL *continue to distract themselves with hair spray, curling irons, and sharp-bristled brushes.*

HOMER: Because that's what we do! Because we're Notes!

No ugly sound will e'er escape our throats!

DANTE: We can't stand hearing language that is crude,

Like "Say, man," "Aw, your mudder!" or "Hey, dude!"

WILLIAM: Please, Dante, spare us hearing those harsh sounds!

We hear enough from *there*, beyond the bounds!

The fact is, poetry remains the test;

Whoever speaks it obviously is best.

SPIKE *and* PUNCH *become more agitated as they hear themselves talked about.*

SPIKE: You hear dat? We gonna just stand here and take abuse from those gags?

PUNCH *(enraged)*:   Best! They think they're best.

> BUZZ, *still focused on* LUCINDA, *tries to quiet his buddies with a wave of his hand. Meanwhile, in* NOTES *territory, the three couples continue whispering in poetry.*

MOLL: Crude! They called us crude!

BETTE: They say we make ugly sounds! They got a lotta nerve!

DOT: Harsh! They better watch who they're calling harsh!

> *Now* THE NOTES *can be heard speaking aloud again.* BUZZ *is completely fascinated with* LUCINDA *now, so his former hostility has fizzled out.*

LUCINDA: Well, language is important, I agree,
            But not the *only* thing, it seems to me. . . .

GUINEVERE *(disagreeing)*:   A crime, when people don't
                  know how to speak—
               Their diction careless and their grammar
               weak.

DESIREE: And slang's another thing that I deplore;
I'd much prefer a lovely metaphor.

HOMER: Lucinda's new here; she will come to see
That perfect speech is a necessity.

*From the other side of the fence come rude
snorts and hoots from* SPIKE *and* PUNCH. BUZZ
is still entranced by LUCINDA. *From here on
there is open verbal combat. Each remark is
answered by the other side. All the males except*
BUZZ *seem about to scale the fence and get at
the enemy. The females, except* LUCINDA, *egg
the males on.*

DANTE *(throwing up his hands in dismay)*: Those piglike
noises from the other side
Are sounds I can't in any way abide.

SPIKE: Poetry—Peeeuuuu!

WILLIAM *(dropping his flowers in shock)*: We can't stand
by and hear ourselves maligned
By boors and ruffians of this vicious kind!

MOLL *(to* SPIKE, PUNCH, *and* BUZZ*)*: Hey, guys, aren't-
cha gonna fight? Where's yuh pride? Where's yuh
guts? Are ya Grunts or aren'tcha?

HOMER *(to Lucinda)*: You see? They're always first
to sling the mud.

And that's not all—they're really out for
blood.

SPIKE: Blood! Dj'hear that? They just said they want
our blood! Come on! We gotta waste 'em, man!
(He tugs at BUZZ'*s shirt, but* BUZZ *waves him away.)*

PUNCH: Whatsamatta, Buzzie baby? Sompin' both-
erin' ya? Ya sick?

By now BUZZ *is sick—lovesick at the mere
sight of* LUCINDA. *Ignoring his fellow* GRUNTS,
*he continues to worship her through the peep-
hole.*

GUINEVERE: They say we're sick. I can't believe their
gall.

Before we know it, they will scale the
wall!

WILLIAM *(drawing everyone—except* LUCINDA, *who holds
back—into a huddle)*: The best defense is
*off*ense. Let's attack.

Let's plan a way to get them from the back.

SPIKE *(drawing everyone—except* BUZZ, *who holds back—
into a huddle)*: Youse guys! Ferget Buzzie! He must

be sick. Meanwhile they're gonna sneak up on us from da rear! Let's beat 'em to it. Come on! *(He leads all the* GRUNTS *except* BUZZ *offstage left.)*

HOMER *(rallying* THE NOTES, *except* LUCINDA, *and leading them offstage right)*: No time to waste.
They're charging from the rear!
A confrontation's imminent, I fear!

As soon as everyone else has gone, BUZZ *scales the wall and stands shyly but admiringly before* LUCINDA, *who smiles at him.*

BUZZ: Hi.

LUCINDA: Hi. Who are you? I feel we've met before.

BUZZ: Yeah? *(Grins and comes closer.)* Buzz's m'name. Lucinda?

LUCINDA *(nodding)*: Are you a Grunt? You're not so bad, I'd say.
So strange, that all The Notes have run away.

BUZZ: They're about to beat on us. They think they're better than us.

LUCINDA: They only want to talk in poetry;
That's not so big a crime, if you ask me.

BUZZ *(backing off)*: You're one of *them*.

LUCINDA: No, no, or if I am, it's accident.
I like you, too. Now tell me where they went.

BUZZ *(suspicious, but can't help being drawn to her)*:
Like, Grunts and Notes, we hate each others' guts. . . .

LUCINDA: You think they treat you like a bunch of mutts.

BUZZ: Yeah! *(Pauses.)* Wait a minute. You *are* one of them! You talk like they do!

LUCINDA: Don't mean to. Just that I have been with them. . . .

BUZZ *(approaching her slowly and taking both her hands in his)*: It don't matter. Talk however you want. June, moon, spoon, the whole bit, don't matter to me. Just so I— Just so we can see each other. Alone. I ain't never felt like this before.

LUCINDA: I want to see you, too—we'll find a way.
It won't be easy— *(Catching herself, she breaks out of iambic pentameter.)* They consider me one of them—a Note. Homer has already asked me to the prom.

BUZZ: No! Tell him no! You can't go with one of them show-offy gags! You aren't like them!

LUCINDA: I know. I know I'm not. I'm just myself.

BUZZ *(taking her in his arms)*: Let's get outta here. Let's get away from alla this.

> *Muttering voices behind the backdrop become louder and escalate into a shouting match between the two gangs. Scuffling sounds are heard, and* BUZZ *and* LUCINDA *listen in horror.*

PUNCH: Yur mudder talks broken English! *(Scuffle, pow, pow!)*

DANTE: No insult could be worse than that to me! You'll pay for that, you Grunt, just wait and see! *(Wham! Crack!)*

DOT: Get 'im, Punch! Tear that gaggy lace off his shirt! *(Pow! Bang! Slam!)*

GUINEVERE: Help, help! What's that they have inside that bag?
Oh, no! They're going to tie us with a gag!

SPIKE: Yeah, gags to finally keep these gaggy kids quiet! Every Grunt's going to catch a Note and tie their mouth shut for good!

A chase begins backstage and ends onstage,
GUINEVERE *and* DESIREE *are already gagged*
when they appear, the captives of THE GRUNTS,
but HOMER, DANTE, *and* WILLIAM *are putting*
up a good fight. BUZZ *pulls* LUCINDA *out of*
danger, and it is at this point that HOMER,
struggling to keep the gag off his mouth, sees
BUZZ *and* LUCINDA *together for the first time.*
He sputters with anger, and when he speaks,
there is a temporary halt to the rumble.

HOMER: Unhand her, villain! Woman, come to me.

BUZZ *(holding on to Lucinda firmly)*: I'm not handing
her over to no gaggy poet.

HOMER: Lucinda, tell him you belong with us.

LUCINDA *(confused)*: I'm not so sure I do—why all
the fuss?

HOMER *(striding threateningly toward Buzz)*: Unhand
her, or your life is on the line;
I'm quite prepared to risk the loss of mine.

Each gang now rallies behind its leader—i.e.,
behind HOMER *and* BUZZ, *who face each other,*
ready for combat, WILLIAM *and* DANTE *untie*
the gags of GUINEVERE *and* DESIREE, *murmurs*

of encouragement are heard on both sides, and then, simultaneously, HOMER *and* BUZZ *throw punches at each other.*

LUCINDA *(intervening between them——to* HOMER):
This can't be happening. No way it can
Whoever wants my love must be a *man*.
(To BUZZ): Look, violence is ridiculous. If
you can't settle this peacefully, I have
an idea. You two have a fair fight—a wrestling
match, for instance. Whoever wins, I'll go out
with—for the time being, anyway.

DANTE: A wrestling match! How vulgar, like TV!

WILLIAM: A duel with swords is what the fight
should be.

PUNCH: Nah. A street fight, and right now, fighting
only with what we got on us.

PUNCH *whispers to* SPIKE *and* BUZZ, *who pull
out of their pockets weapons such as pocket
knives and beer can openers.* THE GRUNTS *girls
prepare to use their hair spray cans, curling
irons, and brushes as weapons. All* THE GRUNTS
stand armed and ready.

DESIREE: That isn't fair—we never carry arms.
Our only armor's our poetic charms.

LUCINDA *(to* THE NOTES, *desperately, as a way of stalling
the fighting)*: So flip a coin before you start to fight.
Whoever wins will choose the weapon,
right?
(To THE GRUNTS*)*: Hey, come on, you guys. Please
let's settle this without anybody getting hurt!

BUZZ: Fair enough, what you just said. *(Throws her
a quarter.)* Flip the coin. Heads, they pick the
weapon; tails, we pick. Whatever weapon gets
picked, it's me against him *(pointing to* HOMER*)*.
Winner walks off with Cindy, and nobody, no
Note and no Grunt, stands in the way.

HOMER: Her name's Lucinda, Grunt—let's get it
right!
Why, that alone is cause enough to fight!

LUCINDA *(coming between them)*: Now, Homer, where
is it you think you're goin'?
Agree that you will let me flip the coin.

*Each gang gets into a huddle to discuss this
suggestion. Coming out of their huddles,
HOMER and BUZZ both nod their agreement*

to the terms. LUCINDA *stands apart, nervously fingering the quarter and eyeing the two gang leaders.*

LUCINDA: I like you both. This tears me up, I swear! I hate to flip the coin. . . .

HOMER: Come on, fair's fair.

THE GRUNTS: Come on, flip! Hurry up! Whatcha waitin' for?

LUCINDA *(Flips the coin)*: Heads.

THE NOTES, *cheering because they have won the toss, regroup into their huddle, while* THE GRUNTS *slouch awkwardly, waiting to hear about the choice of weapons. After a second* HOMER *comes triumphantly out of the huddle.*

HOMER: We've found the perfect way to kill you birds.
The weapon we are choosing will be . . . words!

GRUNTS: Huh? Wha—? Come off it! Punkin' sissies—*words?*

LUCINDA: Words?

WILLIAM *(smugly)*: Yes, words as weapons; words will win the day!
> The pen is stronger than the sword, they say.

GUINEVERE: We'll stage a battle, all in poetry,
> Whoe'er performs the best claims victory.

SPIKE: Hey, wha—?

PUNCH: No punkin' fair!

BETTE, DOT, MOLL: They'll kill us fer sure!

HOMER *(gloating)*: Each group will write a verse, and when we're done,
> Then Buzz and I'll recite them, one on one.

BUZZ: Ya mean I gotta beat him at recitin' a punkin' *poem*?

BETTE: We gotta *write* it first—that's worse!

SPIKE: Forget it. *(Pulls out his knife.)* We changed our minds. Street fight—that's what we want.

BUZZ *(smiling shyly at Lucinda)*: Nah. We agreed. We got our pride. We'll do it—we're Grunts!

PUNCH: How long is a poem?

DESIREE: A poem has no set length and no set form;
For sonnets, fourteen lines would be the norm.

MOLL: *Sonnets?* What's she talkin', Greek?

GUINEVERE: Although a poem doesn't have to rhyme,
Rhymed couplets are, I think, the most sublime.

DOT: Rhymed *what?*

BUZZ: Hey. Okay, so we—we'll write a poem. And I'll say it. How do we know who wins? It can't be up to you gags.

HOMER: We, of course, will judge—don't mean to boast,
But certainly it's clear—we know the most.

SPIKE: No punkin' fair!

LUCINDA: He's right. It isn't fair. You can't compete and judge at the same time. There's only one fair way to do it. After both sides have written their verses, we'll call in an outside audience and let them make a decision by the length and loudness of their applause.

WILLIAM: The audience may not be in the know;
           They might like comic books instead of
           Poe.

BETTE: Tough jelly beans! That's the chance you take! We'll get our tightest friends to be the audience.

DESIREE: *Our* friends will gladly come to help us out.
           True poetry will win without a doubt.

BUZZ: How long we got to come up with this thing?

LUCINDA *(thinking fast)*: We'll get permission to call for an audience over the football field loudspeaker, and while kids are gathering here, you'll write your words. It might be hard, though, to have a contest here, with this wall in the way. Maybe we should take it down.

PUNCH: Take the wall down? So what'll we look through, when we wanta see what they're doin'? *(SPIKE punches him for his stupidity.)*

DANTE: The wall protects us from gross sights and
           sound.
           For just this contest, though, let's take it
           down.

BUZZ *and* HOMER *assess the feelings of their groups and then nod reluctantly at* LUCINDA.

LUCINDA: I'd love to see the wall come down right now. Let's do it! Which of you can show us how?

Everybody from both gangs kicks and pushes until the wall topples. At first they are all gleeful, but then, remembering they're supposed to be enemies, they regroup into opposing gangs.

LUCINDA *(aside)*: Regardless of how things turn out, I, for one, hope never to see that wall again. *(To both gangs)* I'm going to get permission to make the announcement over the loudspeaker. While I'm gone, get busy. Ready, get set, write!

As both gangs dive into huddles, on their own turf, and furiously begin to organize and create, LUCINDA *exits and the stage goes dark. Within a few seconds the announcement blares.*

AMPLIFIED VOICE: Attention! We'll announce this
only once—
A showdown, now, between The
Notes and Grunts.
For once and all, these enemies
will clash;

Come running, now, to hear who
wins this bash.

Hey, all you students, and jocks, and streetwise
guys and gals. Book over here, ya hear? The verbal
rumble is on. We need ya to listen up good and put
these gangs to the test to figure out which of 'em
is best.

*A few extras come from behind the curtain and
sit down among the actual audience to create
the illusion of an audience gathering. The stage
lights up again, and* LUCINDA *reappears at
stage center. She shouts "Stop writing!" and
both gangs follow her orders. The two leaders
prepare to face off on the spot where the wall
was, and their respective gangs are seated behind
them, ready to cheer them on.* LUCINDA *supervises the flipping of a coin to determine who
will go first.*

LUCINDA: Heads it is—The Notes will go first.
Okay, the contest's ready to begin.
Good luck to both, and may the best
gang win.

*At this point the two original actor-written
verses are delivered, the first by* HOMER *and*

the second by BUZZ. *After both poems have been recited,* LUCINDA *calls for applause from the actual audience, and she determines who the winner is. She then holds up his arm, as in a championship boxing match, and she walks off the stage with him, followed by both gangs, who accept the results peacefully. The curtain falls on a quiet school yard with no dividing wall.*

CURTAIN

ROBIN F. BRANCATO

Always wanting to be a writer "for as long as I can remember," Robin F. Brancato published her first novel—*Don't Sit Under the Apple Tree*—in 1975 after working as a copyeditor and then as an English teacher. Since then, her teaching experiences and her students have provided the major influences on her writing. *Winning* is a story about a star football player's paralyzing injury and how a sensitive teacher helps him deal with his life. *Come Alive at 505* is the story of a boy who wants to become a radio disc jockey. *Uneasy Money*, her most recent novel, follows the suddenly disrupted life of an eighteen-year-old boy who wins the New Jersey lottery but has trouble managing his millions.

Brancato's other novels for young adults include *Something Left to Lose*, a story about the influence of astrology on the friendship among three girls; *Sweet Bells Jangled out of Tune*, a novel in which a high school teenager learns how to deal with her senile grandmother; and *Blinded by the Light*, a look at religious cults that was made into a Movie of the Week. *Facing Up* deals with the relationship between two high school friends, their mutual attraction to the same girl, and the death of one of them in a car accident.

Before she wrote *War of the Words*, Robin Brancato's experience with theater included acting in minor roles in high school and college plays, being the first woman to write lyrics for the all-male Mask and Wig Show at the University of Pennsylvania, and being a lifelong theatergoer. She currently teaches creative writing at Teaneck (New Jersey) High School and is working on a new novel.

DONALD R. GALLO

Although he almost always had a lead role in elementary school plays as well as church pageants, Don Gallo's dramatic interests ended abruptly one Easter Sunday when he was unable to recall a single word from a memorized passage he was attempting to recite at the morning church service. Any theatrical talents he may possess have since been utilized only in English classrooms and lecture halls.

Dr. Gallo, who has been a junior high school English teacher and reading specialist, is a professor of English at Central Connecticut State University, where he supervises student teachers and teaches courses in writing and in literature for young adults. He lives in West Hartford, Connecticut.

He has edited three collections of short stories written by famous writers of books for young adults; *Sixteen*, *Visions*, and *Connections*; and he has written a critical biography of author Richard Peck. His most recent book is a collection of autobiographies of notable young adult authors called *Speaking for Ourselves*.